SHOPACHECK'S RUGBY LEAGUE REVIEW 1986

SHOPACHECK'S RUGBY LEAGUE REVIEW 1986

ff
faber and faber
LONDON · BOSTON

First published in 1986 by
Faber and Faber Limited
3 Queen Square London WC1N 3AU

Photoset and printed in Great Britain by
Redwood Burn Limited, Trowbridge, Wiltshire

British Library Cataloguing in Publication Data

Shopacheck's rugby league review.
1. Rugby football—Periodicals
796.33′3′05   GV944.8

ISSN 0269–3240
ISBN 0–571–14688–0

Contents

Acknowledgements

All the photographs in this book, except two, are published by kind permission of the Andrew Varley Picture Agency. The exceptions are no.25 from Phil Callaghan and no.26 from Eddie Rolmanis.

1

THE INTERNATIONAL SEASON

Anyone who thought that the 1985–86 international season would be simply an appetizer for the impending 1986 Ashes series against Australia would have been very much mistaken. Though the initial stages of the new World Cup competition were hardly likely to create the same level of sudden-death excitement that will be more evident as the tournament nears its climax in 1988, the Tests against New Zealand and France provided a level of drama, footballing excellence and spellbinding intensity rarely experienced before in international Rugby League.

On a memorable November afternoon at Elland Road, Leeds, Great Britain's international rehabilitation was seen to be nearly complete when Lee Crooks's last-minute penalty sailed between the posts to square the series against New Zealand after over 240 minutes of unrelenting combat. Great Britain, regarded as underdogs before the Kiwis arrived, had achieved immense progress on the field, and created a wave of national pride and emotional support in the process. Not only did that Elland Road Test attract a crowd of 22,209 paying spectators – the highest attendance to watch an Anglo–New Zealand international since the Kiwis' 1961 tour – but no less than nine million British television sets were tuned in to live coverage of the game.

The overall excellence of the Great Britain–New Zealand Test series dominated the season in England. It was the first home series between Great Britain and a touring team to be played since the sixth-tackle 'turnover' rule had been introduced with such positive results, and it was also the first home series since the invincible 1982 Kangaroos had swept through Britain and France with such devastating effect. Perhaps even more significantly, it was the first home series since the relaxation of the ban on international transfers which had allowed Australian players to play such a dominating and constructive role in the League's domestic competitions.

Incredibly, the influx of overseas players into British clubs had, and still has, its critics – people who try to divert attention from their own inadequacies by suggesting that importing foreign players stunts the development of local talent. Quite the reverse has been the case as numerous Australian and New Zealand players have stamped their individual skills on the performances of just about every successful British club, and in doing so have greatly encouraged local players, particularly the younger ones, to develop the same dedicated attitude towards their sport demanded by the high-pressure environment of Rugby League in Sydney and Brisbane.

Have British clubs become too reliant on overseas talent? Or has the presence of the imports helped British players improve their own standards to the point where the Great Britain national team can, once again, compete confidently at the highest level of Test football? Back in 1982, after the ban had for five solid years effectively prevented any dialogue between the League clubs of Britain and Australia and the Sydney competition gathered pace in so many directions, the British national team's standards had dropped considerably below those in the southern hemisphere.

Now Great Britain's fine achievements against New Zealand in October and November suggested, quite dramatically, that that was no longer the case. Even more startling was the impact made by two young individuals on Great Britain's victorious second Test and drawn third Test performances against the Kiwis – Garry Schofield and Lee Crooks. Of numerous British players who joined Australian clubs in the summer of 1985, only Schofield and Crooks were major successes. Sydney football brought the best out of the Hull pair, and Crooks, especially, returned a much more mature, effective player. His qualities were seen at their best in a towering performance that paved the way for Great Britain's comeback in the 6–6 draw with New Zealand, and later in another commanding front-rower's display in the 24–10 victory over France at Wigan. Schofield, meanwhile, spent his months in the Balmain back-line sharpening his already magnetic instinct for support play to such a fine pitch that it seemed almost inevitable that, one day, he would explode on to all the right passes, into all the right gaps, at all the right times. It finally happened on Saturday 2 November at Central Park, as the young centre ran in all four Great Britain tries in the 25–8 win over New Zealand.

That victory wasn't just a series leveller for Britain; it was a major turning point, a day when self-confidence came back to the British team. Self-respect had already returned in the first Test at Headingley two weeks before when, although the Kiwis had won 24–22 and looked the stronger side in the process, Britain had gone within a whisker of glory and shown that, in Ellery Hanley, they possessed an individual running back with such immense flair and power that they could create tries from any part of the field.

While in the final analysis it might have appeared that it was the individual talents of such as Hanley and Schofield, followed by the ice-cool goal-kicking of Lee Crooks, that enabled Great Britain to achieve their win, draw and near-miss against New Zealand, the truth was that the platform for success had been achieved as a result of the meticulous planning and preparation masterminded by the coach, Maurice Bamford, and his assistant, Phil Larder.

Great Britain had named a squad to train on through the summer of 1985, and the team came together to spend five days at the National Sports Centre at Lilleshall in August. It was in those five days that Maurice Bamford started the process of building up the 'family' team spirit that was to be a focal point of his motivational methods. The players themselves elected Harry Pinner as the man they wanted as their team captain, and peripheral ideas aimed at increasing patriotic fervour, such as parading a Union Jack before the crowd at Test matches, were formulated. Such things might not have been to everybody's taste, but they certainly had the desired effect in building up vibrant vocal support from the public.

Maurice Bamford, in his second season as international coach, always pinned great store on 'pride' and 'commitment'. An emotional man, with a burning enthusiasm for Rugby League, Bamford learned a lot from his initial year as Great Britain coach. Fiercely proud, but never too proud to learn or to seek advice from outside sources, he had sampled an invigorating first Test win against France, followed by an equally deflating loss to the same opponents in 1984–85. However, this was followed by a third game against France in a special 'challenge' match staged in blazing sunshine at Limoux on 1 June. The game was staged as a memorial to two much admired French journalists, who had recently died, Alex Angel and Guy Cassayet, and pitched a President's XIII against a British XIII.

While the French team may have treated this as a light-hearted end-of-season friendly, and, indeed, found themselves in some disarray with the resignation of their coach Raymond Gruppi and manager Jean Panno in the week leading up to the game, Maurice Bamford was offered, and was delighted to accept, the opportunity of using the trip to Limoux as a fully-fledged trial match for his Great Britain players.

The British XIII won comfortably 46–8, with Ellery Hanley adding no less than five more tries to take his total for the season to an amazing sixty! Bamford and his assistant, Phil Larder, however, were later to admit just how instructive the whole exercise had been, in particular their introduction of forwards John Fieldhouse and Ian Potter to the national team squad. Neither Fieldhouse nor Potter had played in the two earlier Tests against France, yet both were to play major roles in the following games with New Zealand.

Bamford visited Australia and New Zealand in the summer of 1985, where he watched the Trans-Tasman Test series as well as a State of Origin match and numerous other local games. The impression made on the British coach was clearly noticeable when he got home. The rhetoric was less euphoric, and carried a much stronger air of realism. Bamford had been impressed by the quality of football he saw, and, possibly, a little shell-shocked by the sheer physical intensity of it all. He knew then, more than ever, the size of the task that lay ahead of Great Britain against the 1985 Kiwis. That the British coped so well against New Zealand was a credit to Bamford's work. The secret of being able to compete at this high level of Rugby League is to be able to play controlled football; to build a solid defensive pattern and maintain discipline when in possession, thus creating the offensive platform on which the runners and the players with flair can launch their attacks.

After the departure of the Kiwis, the annual clashes with France, at senior, Under-21, and Colts levels came along to keep Britain's momentum flowing. The Colts enjoyed almost total dominance over their French counterparts but, for the first time, the Under-21s did not have things their own way against the Espoirs or 'young hopefuls'. A stunning defeat at St Estève was followed by a close match in the return fixture at Whitehaven, leaving the young Frenchmen to take greater satisfaction from their season. Several of those Espoirs went on to make their senior Test debuts as France surprised a disappointing Great Britain side with a 10–10 draw in the World Cup fixture at Avignon.

France themselves made a great deal of progress during the season. In a revolutionary move, they appointed the Australian Tas Baitieri as international team coach. His task of rebuilding credibility in world terms for French RL, and perhaps even more important, of rebuilding the sport's own credibility with the French nation, was, and still is, immense. But Baitieri set about the job with enthusiasm and sound logic – the very qualities that have built the success of the game in Australia. After taking stock in two Tests against New Zealand, in both of which France competed with spirit, only to suffer morale-sapping 22–0 defeats, Baitieri got to work with the country's young players, his only realistic hope of building a new, more optimistic, more disciplined attitude to Rugby League in a country where the game is currently firmly in the rut of being viewed as a minority sport.

THE KIWI TOUR
THE NEW ZEALANDERS IN BRITAIN

The eleventh New Zealand touring team to come to Europe faced a taxing itinerary of twenty games in nine weeks. The tour was billed as the most eagerly-awaited visit ever by a Kiwi side, largely because of the steady stream of excellent results achieved by New Zealand since their memorable 1980 tour of Britain and France and the impact made by those players who had chosen to pursue careers as professionals with British and Australian clubs.

Rugby League is still a largely amateur sport in New Zealand, and since 1980 the NZRL have actively encouraged their players, once they have given good service to their country in Tests, to play for professional clubs overseas. That new experience, largely aided by the calm, mature approach of the New Zealand national coach, Graham Lowe, has seen the Kiwis emerge as real rivals to Australia as Rugby League's world champions.

Lowe took over from Cecil Mountford as Kiwi coach in 1983. That year, New Zealand were desperately unlucky to lose to Australia in Auckland, before achieving a memorable victory at Brisbane's Lang Park, thereby ending Australia's dominance of Test football. Later, the Kiwis followed up with a record-breaking Test win over Papua New Guinea. In 1984, they achieved their first-ever 3–0 series win over Britain, setting the stage for 1985 to be, potentially, the greatest year in the history of New Zealand Rugby League.

In the event, the record books will show that the 1985 Kiwis did not achieve immortality. A last-minute try by John Ribot cost them the series against Australia, and a last-minute penalty-goal by Lee Crooks meant that they had to share the glory against Great Britain. Only against France was the series won. Nevertheless, New Zealand led the World Cup table as they flew home from Europe, with two wins and a draw from their three matches played. Those points already on the board may prove vital in the final reckoning.

The 1985 Kiwis brought twenty-four players to their British base at Harrogate. There were eleven newcomers to international RL in the squad captained by Mark Graham, who became the first man in history to lead a second Kiwi tour to Europe. In addition to Graham, five of the twenty-four were attached to professional clubs in Sydney: Bell, McGahan, Filipaina and the Sorensen brothers. The touring party consisted of:

Backs: Dean Bell (Eastern Suburbs, Sydney), Mark Bournville (Mount Albert, Auckland), Shane Cooper (Mount Albert, Auckland), Mark Elia (Te Atatu,

Auckland), Olsen Filipaina (Eastern Suburbs, Sydney), Clayton Friend (Manukau, Auckland), Glen Gibb (Runanga, West Coast), Shane Horo (Waring City Tigers, Waikato), Vaun O'Callaghan (Huntly South, Waikato), Ron O'Regan (City Newton, Auckland), Joe Ropati (Otahuhu, Auckland), Darrel Williams (Mount Albert, Auckland).

Forwards: Ricky Cowan (Mount Albert, Auckland), James Goulding (Richmond, Auckland), Mark Graham (North Sydney), Hugh McGahan (Eastern Suburbs, Sydney), Adrian Shelford (Hornby, Canterbury), Dane Sorensen (Cronulla, Sydney), Kurt Sorensen (Cronulla, Sydney), Sam Stewart (Randwick, Wellington), Howie Tamati (Waitara, Taranaki), Ross Taylor (Hornby, Canterbury), Wayne Wallace (Hornby, Canterbury), Owen Wright (Manukau, Auckland).

While only Mark Graham and hooker Howie Tamati were survivors of the 1980 tour, for the first time the New Zealanders were able to call on their British-based professionals. There were eight players who had all been outstanding members of the 1980 Kiwi team: Gary Kemble, Dane O'Hara, James Leuluai and Fred Ah Kuoi (all Hull), Gary Prohm and Gordon Smith (both Hull KR), Kevin Tamati (Warrington) and Graeme West (Wigan). Those players were contracted for Test duty only, and had the opportunity to play against the tourists for their clubs, which most of them did!

Another significant 'first' was that this New Zealand team arrived as clear favourites to beat both Great Britain and France. Never before had a Kiwi side carried such a tag. Coach Graham Lowe found his 'favourites' label an uneasy burden. He was not pretending when he spoke of the dangers of the British players' flair – a flair that had been evident, even in adversity, when the 1984 Lions had lost in New Zealand. Lowe's fears were to prove well founded in the first and second Tests.

Sadly, the opening match at Wigan was marred by the most appalling rainstorms throughout the game. The weather undoubtedly cut an anticipated crowd of more than 20,000 down to less than 13,000, and severely hampered both teams in their attempts to play football. The New Zealanders, no strangers, of course, to wet conditions, did not adjust well. While Wigan were content to play 'wet-weather football', ably assisted by the Australian Steve Ella continually pumping the ball deep into Kiwi territory, Mark Graham's men were far too adventurous. They looked ominously dangerous, but time after time they fumbled the ball as they tried to put expansive passing movements together at great speed. Wigan just sat back and waited for their visitors to make mistakes, after they had taken an early lead through a Shaun Edwards try. The Kiwis duly obliged, and an 8–14 defeat put an end to any over-confidence there may have been in the tourists' minds.

Odsal Stadium, Bradford, 9 October
Great Britain Under-21 12 New Zealanders 16

The Kiwis' first game on Yorkshire soil brought their first win of the tour, but it was the young Britons who took most of the glory with an excellent performance, inspired by Gary Divorty, which in the end had the New Zealanders hanging on for victory.

On a cold, wet night at Odsal Stadium, a disappointingly small crowd – considering the reputation of the tourists – provided little atmosphere in the huge arena. This was the second year that Britain had fielded a team at Under-21 level since lowering the age restriction from Under-24, and their selection contained many young players who had been outstanding in club competition. Captained by Salford's aggressive hooker, Paul Groves, the Under-21s were not overawed by meeting such experienced opponents as Filipaina, Dane Sorensen, Wright and McGahan, and they played superb football to create a try by Shaun Edwards. It came from a perfectly disguised short pass by Divorty, which sent Andy Dannatt bursting into the clear, Edwards supporting at his shoulder, to put the ball down behind the posts.

The British youngsters trailed 6–16 at one stage, before coming back and putting great pressure on the tourists, in what turned out to be by far the best performance of the season by the Under-21s. For the New Zealanders it was still a nervous-looking display in the eyes of those English observers who remembered the excellence of the 1980 tourists and, perhaps unrealistically, expected Graham Lowe's men merely to press the button and slip into overdrive. It was also a measure of the excellent defensive strategy of the young Britons that the Kiwis could not find the freedom to run on too many occasions.

One significant factor for New Zealand was that their experienced front-rower, Dane Sorensen, came through this match, and the opening game at Wigan, unscathed, putting in a consistent effort both times. This was Dane's first football for many months after undergoing major surgery on his knee, and his presence would be required in the more demanding Tests ahead.

Great Britain Under-21: Lyon (Widnes); Dalton (Whitehaven), Creasser (Leeds), Forster (Warrington), Carbert (Warrington); Edwards (Wigan), Ford (Wigan); Dannatt (Hull), Groves (Salford), Wane (Wigan), Powell (Leeds), Lyman (Featherstone Rovers), Divorty (Hull)

Substitutes: Westhead (Leigh) for Lyman after 35 minutes, David Hulme (Widnes) for Creasser after 46 minutes

Scorers: tries – Edwards, Forster; goals – Carbert (2)

New Zealanders: Williams; Bournville, Ropati, Filipaina, Horo; Cooper, Gibb; Dane Sorensen, Wallace, Goulding, Wright, Stewart, McGahan

Substitutes: Kurt Sorensen for Dane Sorensen after 47 minutes, O'Regan not used

Scorers: tries – McGahan, Horo; goals – Filipaina (4)

Referee: D. Fox (Wakefield)

Attendance: 2,285

From the cold of Odsal, and the wet of Wigan, the Kiwis finally emerged into some sunshine for their third match, at Craven Park, against the reigning league champions, Hull Kingston Rovers. The Hull KR side contained two New Zealanders, Gary Prohm and Gordon Smith, as well as Australians Dorahy and Miller. Smith played superbly in the first half, in direct confrontation with his Test rival Clayton Friend, but was forced to retire with a damaged ankle. Meanwhile, Prohm impressed his old mentor at Otahuhu, Graham Lowe, so much that it seemed he had booked a Test place there and then. Hull KR gave the Kiwis tough opposition, and it was only a controversial try in the second half scored by the former Kent and Southend Invicta centre, Mark Elia, that put the tourists in the driving seat. Throughout the game, the New Zealanders' inexperienced backs looked uncomfortable but the calm assurance of their captain, Mark Graham, playing one of his few full games of the tour, guided the Kiwis to a deserved 20–10 victory.

The former Barrow player, Ron O'Regan, captained the tourists as they romped home, 32–6, against Cumbria, a side composed entirely of second-division players. There was more local interest in the appearance of Dean Bell in his first game of the tour after completing a nine-week suspension imposed by the New South Wales authorities. Bell, as a twenty-year-old, had played for Carlisle, and actually represented Cumbria county against the 1982 Australians. On this occasion, his incisive pace played a big part in Cumbria's disappointing defeat, on a pleasant evening, before a surprisingly large crowd of over 5,000. The match in this northerly outpost of the League was a confidence booster for the Kiwis' young newcomers, as thoughts turned to the more serious business of the first Test.

First Test
Headingley, Leeds, 19 October
Great Britain 22 New Zealand 24

What a great game! The first Test in the series sponsored by Whitbread provided a feast of brilliant attacking Rugby League, surrounded by no little drama and controversy. Few people at the Headingley ground that Saturday afternoon could not have left the ground emotionally drained as the final whistle was blown by the Australian referee, Barry Gomersall. Great Britain lost the game, but won back much self-belief.

No less than nine of Great Britain's thirteen had been members of the unsuccessful 1984 Lions touring team; the difference was in the management and coaching. Maurice Bamford had adopted a positive approach, was prepared to give attacking players their head, and was adamant that: 'We can win, and we must win'.

Graham Lowe surprised English observers by selecting James Leuluai at full-back ahead of his Hull team-mate, Gary Kemble, but it wasn't an entirely unexpected move as it simply meant that the Kiwis started with the same combination they had had against Australia after Kemble had been taken from the field injured. Leuluai was no stranger to the full-back role, and his selection was aimed at providing more penetration in attack. But in the opening seconds New Zealand were left to rue the absence of the reliable Kemble as, in Great Britain's first attack, their skipper, Harry Pinner, launched a bomb. Leuluai failed to take the ball, a mad scramble ensued in the in-goal area and, after consultation with his touch-judge, Mr Gomersall awarded the touchdown to Andy Goodway. Mick Burke converted and Britain were six points up and away to a dream start.

For a few moments the crowd, eager to cheer every British action, was buoyant as Great Britain basked in the glory of being in the lead against a side described as the best Test team in the world. After thirty minutes, however, the mood had changed completely. The Kiwi defence had sized up the situation, got the measure of Harry Pinner in the centre of the field, thus rendering Britain's forward attack ineffective, and cut loose themselves with a series of lightning raids. Three tries in quick succession, one converted, put the Kiwis 14–6 ahead and seemingly in complete control.

Through all this, Mark Graham strode like a colossus. The British defence could not handle him. Little did we know that this would be the last time we would see a fully-fit Mark Graham in action on this tour. One can only ponder on what might have happened had Graham stayed uninjured, for in those thirty minutes of the first Test he made a deep impression on everybody there.

1 The first Test against New Zealand ended in defeat for Britain by just two points. Here Lee Crooks, the Great Britain prop forward, is half tackled by the Kiwi captain, Mark Graham, with Gary Prohm in support. In the third Test it was Lee Crooks's last-minute penalty from way out on the touchline that squared the match and the series.

In the seconds leading up to half-time there occurred two incidents, involving the outstanding individual on each side, that illustrated the best and the worst of Rugby League. It was Ellery Hanley who brought Britain back into the game with one of those very special tries that have become his trademark – twisting and turning out of a tackle from a virtual standing start to make a touchdown out of nothing. That was the flair that Graham Lowe had been worried about. It was impossible to predict, impossible to stop, and better was yet to come. On a less palatable note, however, Mark Graham was seriously injured by a blow to the face from Des Drummond. Graham appeared for the second half, visibly in much distress with his face already badly swollen, only to be called from the field almost immediately and replaced by the openly aggressive Kevin Tamati. Suddenly, the Kiwis looked vulnerable. The whole of the second half was to be a backs-to-the-wall effort from them, as Britain's confidence increased, Tony Myler and John Fieldhouse growing in stature as Test players almost by the minute.

The lead changed hands frequently before Britain finally achieved the breakthrough that appeared to have brought them victory. After a strong burst from his own line by Drummond, there was a minor loss of momentum for a split second as Arkwright seemed uncertain where to run, before Hanley took possession and stormed down the mainstand touchline. He shrugged off Leuluai's tackle and, as the Kiwi cover moved in, floated a high, looping pass into the hands of Joe Lydon. Lydon scored like a bullet what seemed a killer try.

Later Maurice Bamford said, 'It was a try fit to win any game.' Most people in the ground probably thought Britain had won the game. They should have had the Kiwis on the ropes: ahead 22–18, three minutes to go, New Zealand without their captain, and down to twelve men with Kevin Tamati in the sin-bin. This was where Britain's young side learned a tough lesson about the realities of Rugby League football at the highest level. For a few seconds, while in possession, Britain lost their discipline as they failed to control the play. A poor clearing kick went straight to Dane O'Hara, the Kiwi defence was not put under pressure as the chase was hesitant, then a missed tackle allowed O'Hara to run the ball straight back into British territory. After a magical pick-up by Gary Prohm, the ball flew right until Kurt Sorensen finally put a pass round the back of a defender for Leuluai to score. Filipaina converted from in front of the posts to make the result 24–22 to New Zealand.

In years to come, this Test match will be talked about as one of the greatest. Defences on both sides were determined and organized, there were few weaknesses, and the tries came from superb attacking play. Undoubtedly, the excellence of that first Test, the spirit and flair of the British performance, and the overall excitement of the contest, set up the remainder of the series. Great Britain had proved they were on the way back.

Great Britain: Burke (Widnes); Drummond (Leigh), Schofield (Hull), Hanley (Wigan), Lydon (Widnes); Myler (Widnes), Fox (Featherstone Rovers); Crooks (Hull), Watkinson (Hull KR), Fieldhouse (Widnes), Goodway (Wigan), Potter (Wigan), Pinner (St Helens)

Substitutes: Arkwright (St Helens) for Crooks after 55 minutes, David Hulme (Widnes) not used

Scorers: tries – Goodway, Hanley, Lydon; goals – Burke (3), Lydon (2)

New Zealand: Leuluai; Bell, Ah Kuoi, Prohm, O'Hara; Filipaina, Friend; Kurt Sorensen, Howie Tamati, Dane Sorensen, Graham, Wright, McGahan

Substitutes: Kemble for Ah Kuoi at half-time, Kevin Tamati for Graham after 41 minutes

Scorers: tries – O'Hara, Bell, Graham, Kurt Sorensen, Leuluai; goals – Filipaina (2)

Referee: B. Gomersall (Australia)

Attendance: 12,591

Four days after the first Test, the tourists' second string faced a stern examination against the Yorkshire county team. Before another disappointing crowd at Odsal Stadium, Bradford, five Test players, Hanley, Schofield, Fox, Crooks and Goodway, gave Yorkshire a formidable look, and, with the Kiwis unhappy at a high penalty count against them, the home side won 18–8. However, the New Zealanders did not seem unduly concerned by the defeat; they were more worried about the chances of Mark Graham regaining fitness in time for the second Test. Mark had been a sorry sight after the first Test. Wearing dark glasses to hide the grotesque swelling to his cheekbone, he was led away to an ambulance and taken to hospital for x-rays. Fortunately, the

2 In Yorkshire's 18–8 victory over the Kiwis, Ellery Hanley, the Yorkshire stand-off, with David Heron in support, is tackled from behind while handing off the Kiwi loose forward, Sam Stewart.

cheekbone was not broken; more serious was the ankle he had turned badly.

Graham was absent as the Kiwis ran up an amazing 46–8 thrashing of St Helens in the seventh game of the tour. It was New Zealand's biggest-ever win on British soil, while Olsen Filipaina's nine goals were also a Kiwi record. St Helens were completely overwhelmed by the speed and power of the visitors' attack, inspired by Friend and Kurt Sorensen, but a blow came when prop forward Ross Taylor sustained a broken arm. Taylor had been in good form, and was pencilled in for a place in the second Test, but now he was to be invalided home and a replacement flown out in the shape of Brent Todd, a young forward from the Linwood club in Christchurch.

When the New Zealanders returned to Headingley to play Leeds a bus strike in the city didn't help the attendance figure, but even allowing for that, a crowd of only 4,713 was a disappointment. Set alongside the two small gatherings at Bradford, one couldn't help realizing how parochial League supporters in West Yorkshire appear to be, the presence of visitors from overseas apparently of far less interest to them than a local club game. Having said that, the Kiwis' 16–10 win over Leeds was not the most entertaining affair of the tour as both sides finished with twelve men, Leeds as a result of injuries, the New Zealanders because winger Mark Bournville had been sent off. He was later cleared by the Rugby League disciplinary committee after a plea of mistaken identity. The fears for Mark Graham grew deeper as Graham Lowe called up Graeme West from Wigan to captain the side against Leeds, eager to get a match under his belt should he be needed for Test duty.

Second Test
Central Park, Wigan, 2 November
Great Britain 25 New Zealand 8

Maurice Bamford took his team into the second Test with confidence. He had seen Great Britain go so close at Headingley that he knew now that victory was no longer just a dream. The first Test had shown just how dangerous his team could be on attack; that they had conceded twenty-four points meant that more work had to go into defence. 'But we don't have to change our game-plan,' said the coach. 'We played the first Test 95 per cent from the heart and only 5 per cent from the head. In Test football you have to do more thinking.'

Great Britain were faced with only one selection problem. Lee Crooks pulled out with an injury, and the problem of finding a suitable replacement

3 Harry Pinner had an excellent series as Britain's captain against New Zealand. Here, in the first Test at Headingley, Leeds, lost by Great Britain 22–24, he breaks from a scrum, evading the tackles of Owen Wright, Mark Graham and Howie Tamati, but pursued now by Dane Sorensen.

emphasized the scarcity of top-class front-rowers in the game, as Britain already had John Fieldhouse, previously regarded as a second-rower, filling the number ten jersey.

After much discussion with his assistant, Phil Larder, Bamford decided to recall the thirty-six-year-old Jeff Grayshon to the national team. It was a controversial choice. Grayshon had been one of the British forwards who had toiled manfully, only to be completely outclassed, against the 1982 Australians, and Bamford had clearly tried to build his teams from younger, more athletic footballers. But Grayshon had continued to be a dominating figure in club Rugby League – in the days leading up to the second Test he was transferred from Bradford Northern to Leeds for whom he played outstandingly well for the rest of the season – and Bamford believed he was the best man for this 'one-off' job.

Jeff Grayshon's selection proved a successful one. His size in the middle of the field took a lot of pressure off skipper Harry Pinner, allowing him to stand much wider off the ruck and probe for the openings that were to unleash Britain's high-speed back division. Everything went right for Great Britain at Central Park, with Fieldhouse dominating up front; scrum-half Deryck Fox proving an excellent link, as well as a remarkably strong first-line tackler; Tony Myler and Ellery Hanley looking dangerous almost every time they carried the ball; and, to crown all this, was Garry Schofield's 'feeling' for a try that took him searing to the line four times, thus equalling the legendary Billy Boston's twenty-one-year-old Test record.

The crowd's reaction to Britain's brilliant finishing was remarkable, as the supporters danced on to the Central Park pitch in delight; Britain's run of ten successive defeats in Tests against Australia and New Zealand had come to an end, and the scene was set for a showdown one week later at Elland Road. New Zealand seemed in disarray. Mark Graham's troublesome ankle did not stand up to a fitness test, and his absence was a serious blow to the Kiwis. Graeme West came in to play on his home ground at Wigan, but, struggling for match fitness, the big second-rower had an unhappy afternoon. Graham Lowe's side had had a disrupted build-up to the Test, but the coach, after his first taste of real failure since becoming national team manager, made no excuses: 'The way we played, the Blind Institute would have beaten us today,' was his succinct comment.

The second Test did not have the same end-to-end drama of the first, or the full-bloodied controversy we were to have in the third. It was too one-sided, too clinical: Great Britain played brilliantly, the Kiwis had a nightmare. Suddenly Britain were the favourites, as the pendulum started to swing. It had all seemed so unlikely before the New Zealanders arrived; now they would be fighting for their footballing lives seven days later in the third Test.

Great Britain: Burke (Widnes); Drummond (Leigh), Schofield (Hull), Hanley (Wigan), Lydon (Widnes); Myler (Widnes), Fox (Featherstone Rovers); Grayshon (Leeds), Watkinson (Hull KR), Fieldhouse (Widnes), Goodway (Wigan), Potter (Wigan), Pinner (St Helens)

Substitutes: Edwards (Wigan) for Burke after 42 minutes, Burton (Hull KR) for Goodway after 55 minutes

Scorers: tries – Schofield (4); goals – Lydon (4); drop goal – Pinner

New Zealand: Kemble; Bell, Leuluai, Prohm, O'Hara; Filipaina, Friend; Kurt Sorensen, Howie Tamati, Dane Sorensen, West, Stewart, McGahan

Substitutes: Ah Kuoi for West after 46 minutes, Cowan for Stewart after 70 minutes

Scorers: try – Bell; goals – Filipaina (2)

Referee: B. Gomersall (Australia)

Attendance: 15,506

As the two Test camps prepared themselves for the Elland Road showdown, the Kiwis first had to overcome the hurdle of Widnes, the most consistently successful club of the last decade. The 'Chemics' did not field any of their Great Britain representatives and presented no great problems to the Kiwis as they swept to a 32–12 victory, their seventh of the tour. The former Widnes player, Kevin Tamati, appeared for the New Zealanders, and made enough impact to re-claim his Test place.

Third Test
Elland Road, Leeds, 9 November
Great Britain 6 New Zealand 6

International Rugby League reached a new peak of public interest in this great epic at Elland Road. It seemed as if the whole country was on tenterhooks as Great Britain, for the first time for as long as anyone could remember, went into this decider as firm favourites. The buzz of expectation on the streets increased when the Kiwi coach Graham Lowe made no less than ten changes. It was a measure of Lowe's positive approach. He didn't pander to what people might say; he 'saw what went wrong, decided on the logical action needed to put it right, and just took that action'.

Out went Howie Tamati after a run of nineteen successive Tests, out went the tour vice-captain Olsen Filipaina and Hugh McGahan; up to loose forward went Gary Prohm, with Fred Ah Kuoi at stand-off, and in came new caps Williams and Wallace. Back, too, was Mark Graham, for only his fourth appearance of the tour. Great Britain knew how much more difficult their second Test win would have been if Graham had been on the field. But what was obvious before this third Test was long underway was that the Kiwi skipper was still far from fit.

Britain could hardly have considered changing their formation after that marvellous victory at Central Park but, significantly as things turned out, Lee Crooks was fit again and claimed one of the substitute roles. Unfortunately, on the morning of the match, Tony Myler had to withdraw with a strained muscle. The Widnes stand-off had been dangerous in the first Test, and absolutely devastating in the second. In the re-shuffle to replace him, Britain's greatest attacking weapon, their three-quarter line, seemed to lose all its menace. Hanley moved to stand-off and couldn't cut loose at all, while his replacement in the centre was Shaun Edwards, who seemed out of his depth at this level of football.

From the start, the ferocity of New Zealand's defence almost rocked the grandstands. It was clear they had decided to put intense physical pressure on the British, and some of the defensive work of Kevin Tamati, Kurt Sorensen and the debutant hooker, Wallace, seemed to border on the illegal several times, raising the wrath of the crowd. But the Kiwis' tactics seemed to be working perfectly as they dominated Great Britain, rendering the home attack powerless. Without Myler, the three-quarters never got into the game, the captain, Harry Pinner, was tackled out of the match, and the British second-rowers could provide no momentum on attack.

Despite the growing waves of New Zealand pressure, Britain's courageous efforts on defence kept them in the game. They stood up to the Kiwi onslaught remarkably well, but one couldn't help thinking that the New Zealanders' work on attack seemed laboured, not for the first time on this tour. The impression was that the incisiveness of Friend, Prohm or Graham could have cut the defence at will, but they never seemed to get the ball going to the right places at the right time.

The home side desperately needed some spark of inspiration, and it came, purely by chance, as a direct result of a New Zealand misdemeanour in the twenty-fifth minute. After Kurt Sorensen had struck Goodway with a high, late blow, earning himself ten minutes in the sin-bin, Goodway was forced to leave the field with concussion, enabling Lee Crooks to take his place in the British pack. Never was a substitution more effective in raising the hopes of a football team.

New Zealand's 6–0 lead at half-time seemed a narrow advantage considering the amount of pressure they had applied. Once again, it was left to Mark Graham to make the break. He had been over the line in the twenty-first minute only to have his 'try' disallowed for failing to ground the ball with sufficient downward pressure; then a smart piece of opportunism enabled the Kiwi skipper to put his team ahead. Tackled just short, he got up and tapped the ball forward with his foot, dropping on it over the line for the touchdown. Many British fans disputed the score, but television replays removed any

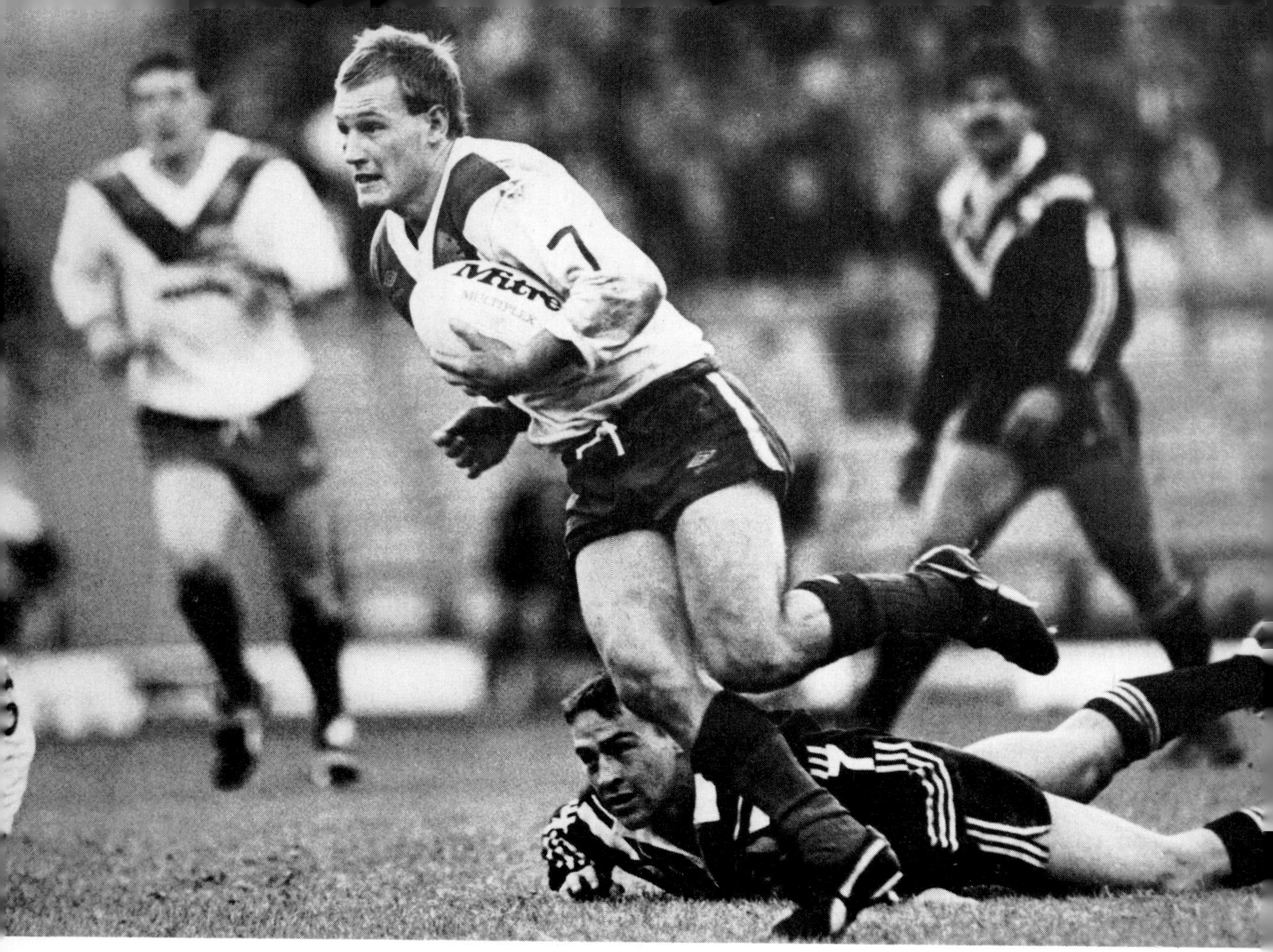

4 Deryck Fox, the Great Britain scrum-half, who enjoyed a fine all-round Test series against New Zealand, evades his opposite number, Clayton Friend, as he starts another British attack.

doubts about its legitimacy. Moreover, they showed that referee Gomersall might well have given an obstruction-try, as Graham, in the act of following his tap forward, was impeded by Fieldhouse coming from an offside position at the play-the-ball.

It was another Graham run, just into the second half, that seemed about to clinch the game for New Zealand, but, miraculously, an interception from Des Drummond saved what looked like a certain try. It was a vital moment in this incredibly exciting Test series. Britain were hanging on for dear life at that point, but then fought back with great courage.

Crooks by this time was by far Britain's most dangerous forward, and it was his sure goal-kicking that turned two penalties into four points, and only a two-point margin between the sides. The tension, which had always been considerable, now built to almost unbearable proportions. The forward battle was of monumental intensity. But New Zealand, angered by a penalty count that by the end of the game had reached 20–7 against, and by the continual intrusions on to the field of play by one of the touch-judges, were seething with frustration. It was perhaps inevitable that some kind of explosion of temper would occur, and after Drummond had fuelled the flames by feigning injury and inviting the touch-judge to react once more, a scrum broke up with both sets of forwards trading blows, as the game moved into its final quarter.

Referee Barry Gomersall was to receive much criticism for his failure to take immediate action to halt the fighting players at the scrum, but British coach Maurice Bamford was not among them. 'Mr Gomersall visually had the scene under control all the time,' said Bamford. 'He knew the fight was going on, but the referee continued the game in the typical Australian manner; he allowed advantage to Great Britain because we had possession and might well have scored or got into a scoring position while this fight was going on.'

The so-called brawl brought a lot of adverse publicity for Rugby League from those areas of the media looking for sensation. Those commentators with a greater understanding of the game recognized that it was just one minute in 240 of incredibly high-pressure football, with much national pride at stake, and with the tension finally getting the better of just a few players on each side. It seemed that New Zealand had weathered the storm, and that Great Britain would have to be content to be gallant losers when, less than two minutes from the end of the series, the same touch-judge went galloping on to the field to draw Mr Gomersall's attention to a swinging arm in a tackle by Prohm. A penalty was given, and Lee Crooks stepped up to take one of the most vital goal-shots of his life. From right on the touchline, on the 'wrong' side for a right-footed instep kicker like Crooks, the substitute forward sent a brilliant kick straight between the posts. Elland Road erupted.

A 6–6 draw brought one World Cup point each, and a squared Test series. For Great Britain, it was as if they had won the World Cup, such was the joy at being back from the international wilderness. More than that, the interest created in international Rugby League had been phenomenal, and could only augur well for the impending visit of the Kangaroos.

Maurice Bamford and his team could take great satisfaction from their efforts against such a well-drilled, tough and talented Kiwi side. 'My overall feelings are that we have progressed slightly,' said Bamford, perhaps trying to keep things in perspective. 'But any progression would have been very, very welcome this time last year.'

John Fieldhouse was selected as Britain's player-of-the-series, and Dane Sorensen was nominated for New Zealand.

Great Britain: Burke (Widnes); Drummond (Leigh), Schofield (Hull), Edwards (Wigan), Lydon (Widnes); Hanley (Wigan), Fox (Featherstone Rovers); Grayshon (Leeds), Watkinson (Hull KR), Fieldhouse (Widnes), Goodway (Wigan), Potter (Wigan), Pinner (St Helens)

Substitutes: Crooks (Hull) for Goodway after 25 minutes, Arkwright (St Helens) for Watkinson after 64 minutes

Scorers: goals – Crooks (3)

New Zealand: Kemble; Williams, Bell, Leuluai, O'Hara; Ah Kuoi, Friend; Kevin Tamati, Wallace, Dane Sorensen, Graham, Kurt Sorensen, Prohm

Substitutes: Filipaina for Ah Kuoi and McGahan for Kevin Tamati after 73 minutes

Scorers: try – Graham; goal – Dane Sorensen

Referee: B. Gomersall (Australia)

Attendance: 22,209

The British section of the Kiwi's tour was not yet over although, after the tensions of the third Test, anything else was sure to be an anti-climax. Heavy frost caused the cancellation of their game against Lancashire at Oldham, before they journeyed to the east coast to bring the curtain down against Hull at the Boulevard. The 1980 tour match against Hull had been one of the most enjoyable occasions of the whole trip, and with Kemble, O'Hara, Leuluai and Ah Kuoi all Hull players, the decision to close the tour at Hull had seemed an admirable move, with more than the promise of a happy carnival atmosphere at the Boulevard. Sadly, it didn't work out that way.

Grabbing centre-stage, referee Gerry Kershaw reacted dramatically and controversially, sending three Kiwis and two Hull players from the field, all before half-time. That ruined the game as a contest, and brought harsh words from the New Zealand management. It was a sad end to a tour that overall seemed to lack the fresh enthusiasm brought by the 1980 Kiwis. Maybe that didn't concern the tourists too much. By 6 o'clock the next morning they had left Harrogate to fly to Paris for the French section of their tour, having achieved a best-ever record against club sides, a shared Test series, and a six-figure profit. The 33–10 win over Hull saw a second replacement player, Marty Crequer, make his first appearance. Crequer, from the Hornby club in Christchurch, was an original selection, but had had to withdraw after sustaining a broken jaw before the team left New Zealand. His place had been taken by Shane Horo, and now Crequer took over from the injured Joe Ropati.

THE NEW ZEALANDERS IN FRANCE

For two days after the Elland Road Test match, Mark Graham could hardly walk. The ankle that he had first injured back in the first Test now required extensive treatment and rest. He flew home to Sydney as the Kiwis went on to France, with Hugh McGahan, and not the tour vice-captain, Olsen Filipaina, taking over the captaincy. It's a sobering thought, but Mark Graham has still, at the time of writing, never been in a series-winning Kiwi side!

The 1985 New Zealanders became the first team from their country to go through a French tour undefeated. In general, they met fairly stiff resistance from the local selections they played. 'They kept coming at us pretty hard in all the games,' summed up Kurt Sorensen, who, more than any other Kiwi, made a big impression on the French. However, the Kiwis' two 22–0 Test victories shattered the French officials, many of whom still fail to understand that the problems of their club championship make the step up to international competition at Test level in the 1980s an enormous one for their players to take. Another blow to officials in the heartlands of French RL came with the shattering 1–66 defeat handed out to the Languedoc–Roussillon selection at Carcassonne. This was the one time the Kiwis overwhelmed their opposition, and it came against a selection from traditionally the strongest area in France.

The narrowest victory for New Zealand was at the Stade de Minimes in Toulouse, against the Midi-Pyrénées selection, where the quality of the local players, notably Gilles Dumas, later to make a big impact in the international arena, surprised the tourists, before they ground out an entertaining 18–12 win. Similarly, an upset was likely when the Kiwis met a Rest of the World XIII at Narbonne. A dreadfully disappointing crowd of only 700 saw a side largely made up of 'Koalas' – Australians playing with French clubs – lead the tourists 10–4 at half-time, before superior conditioning told in the end. This game produced the best football of the tour in France, with the New Zealanders eventually winning 22–10.

Crowds were small throughout the French tour, but there were other reasons for this in addition to the present low-ebb of the game in France. It was deliberate policy to stage matches in or around big cities for media promotional purposes – so the Kiwis played in Paris, Marseilles and near Bordeaux, rather than against local opposition in such strongholds of the game as Avignon, Perpignan or Villeneuve, where bigger, more fanatical crowds would have been guaranteed.

The pleasant surprise for the French Federation was the excellent turnout (almost 2,000 paying spectators) for the match at Talence, near Bordeaux, an area which no longer has a senior Rugby League club. There the Kiwis won 22–10 against an Aquitaine/Provence–Côte d'Azur selection (a bizarre geographical mixture from two areas hundreds of miles apart). In this game, Howie Tamati was given the honour of captaining the New Zealanders in what turned out to be his farewell appearance.

The New Zealanders had been scheduled to open the tour against the French military team, the Bataillon de Joinville. However, in view of the political situation between France and New Zealand in the aftermath of the *Rainbow Warrior* affair, the match was cancelled for diplomatic reasons. Instead, a hastily recruited selection faced the Kiwis on a freezing night at La Cipale in the suburbs of Paris for their first game on French soil – a side built around Paris-based players plus a couple of the Army representatives and several guest players from the south. The tourists defied the cold, and the opposition, to win 20–8 in a good humoured match.

First Test
Stade Velodrome, Marseilles, 23 November
France 0 New Zealand 22

The Kiwis were happy to leave the freezing temperatures of Paris to find bright sunshine and warm breezes drifting in from the Mediterranean as they lined up in Marseilles for the first of two Tests against France. This game came just a fortnight after the epic confrontation at Elland Road, but the atmosphere was in marked contrast.

The staging of the Test at the magnificent Velodrome Stadium drew much criticism. It has a capacity of around 60,000, yet a tiny crowd of less than 1,500 people (including a fair proportion of travelling Kiwi supporters) were huddled together among the rows of empty seats; the lack of atmosphere showed in the play in a match described as a 'Test without passion'. Later it was revealed that there had been only 492 paying spectators at the game, the smallest crowd ever registered at a Test match. The French Federation sacrificed credibility for financial profit by staging both Tests on Saturdays before live television cameras, due in part to an attempt to accommodate New Zealand television who took the games live by satellite. Naturally, that had a catastrophic effect

5 Tas Baitieri, France's new Rugby League national team coach, had the difficult task of rebuilding their international credibility, and, perhaps more important, of rebuilding the sport's own credibility within France. He tackled the job with infectious enthusiasm and no little success. Though France lost both Tests against New Zealand, they earned a highly creditable draw against Britain at Avignon and their Espoirs did exceptionally well to beat Britain in the first Under-21 international.

on attendances but brought in a sizeable, and welcome, profit by way of stadium advertising.

This was France's first international with Tas Baitieri at the helm. Born Bortolo Baitieri, twenty-eight years ago in Sydney (Tas was a school playground nickname that stuck), this highly personable young man was formerly a respected forward in the Sydney Premiership, a captain of Canterbury in the pre-Warren Ryan era. Four years ago he travelled to France to try his luck with the Paris-Châtillon club. Being of Italian parentage, he already had firm European links, and, having mastered the French language, he set about making Châtillon a serious football club with first-division aspirations.

Baitieri's appointment as coach to the national team was a controversial move by President Jacques Soppelsa. Criticism came thick and fast from the traditionalists who were appalled by the presence of a foreigner in charge of the national team. One can imagine the same kind of reaction in Britain in similar circumstances. But French Rugby League was in such a rut that the introduction of an outsider like Baitieri offered them their only hope of ever making real progress in international terms. Tas and his co-coach, Guy Vigouroux, former mentor of the relatively successful French Universities and Junior teams, had little time to do anything before the arrival of the Kiwis in France. Those observers anxious to criticize were given ample scope with the 22–0 defeat at Marseilles.

By this time, the New Zealanders were like a smooth running machine, with the skills of McGahan and the raw power of the Sorensen brothers making their pack a formidably powerful unit. It took them seventeen minutes to break the deadlock at Marseilles, when Kurt Sorensen scored the first of his two tries. Spirited French defence kept the score to only eight points at half-time, and France could easily have been in front had they taken their two clear-cut chances: first Max Chantal, after a bullocking run, was stopped dead in his tracks right under the posts by a brilliant ball-and-all tackle by Kemble, and Chantal lost possession in the process. Then Couston appeared on the opposite flank to create an overlap for Ratier, only to throw out a wild pass behind his unmarked team-mate who had a clear run only feet from the goal-line.

The second half saw New Zealand methodically grind down the French resistance. The Hull quartet of Kemble, Leuluai, O'Hara and Ah Kuoi all played strongly. By the end of the game, the French were well beaten and dispirited. In the final quarter, Yvan Grésèque was called from the field and substituted. In some ways that could be seen as a symbolic gesture, as the old French mentality gave way to Baitieri's attempts to bring more organization and discipline. Grésèque had repeatedly defied his coach's instructions, making it impossible for his team to implement any kind of game-plan. The

Catalan scrum-half could not change his attitude to the game, which was all off-the-cuff improvisation with little concern for team effort. Yvan slouched from the field, probably for the last time in an international match, bringing the curtain down on a Test career that began against the 1978 Kangaroos and had subsequently taken him all round the world in a series of fascinating duels against the top half-backs from every other Rugby League country.

France: Serge Pallarès (XIII Catalan); Ratier (Lézignan), Francis Laforgue (XIII Catalan), Palisses (St Estève), Couston (Le Pontet); Espugna (Lézignan), Gréséque (XIII Catalan); Chantal (Villeneuve), Mantèse (Paris–Châtillon), Titeux (Le Pontet), Montgaillard (XIII Catalan), Palanque (Le Pontet), Guy Laforgue (XIII Catalan)

Substitutes: Andre Pérez (Toulouse) for Gréséque after 73 minutes, Serge Pérez (St Estève) for Palanque after 79 minutes

New Zealand: Kemble; Williams, Bell, Leuluai, O'Hara; Cooper, Friend; Kurt Sorensen, Wallace, Dane Sorensen, Wright, Goulding, McGahan

Substitutes: Ah Kuoi for O'Hara after 42 minutes, Filipaina for Goulding after 59 minutes

Scorers: tries – Kurt Sorensen (2), O'Hara, McGahan; goals – Dane Sorensen (2), Filipaina

Referee: R Campbell (England)

Attendance: 1,500

Second Test
Stade Gilbert Brutus, Perpignan, 7 December
France 0   New Zealand 22

Since the early days of the International Board, the French have always been the ones who really wanted a world cup, and it was they who instigated the latest incarnation which, after being spread over three years, will culminate with a final in Australia in 1988. Therefore, it was only natural that the French should try to promote their first World Cup qualifier on home soil with genuine enthusiasm. The New Zealanders, too, had much to play for as they journeyed to Perpignan for the final game of their long and arduous European tour.

With the cold of winter firmly entrenched in northern England, there are few more pleasant cities to which to retreat to watch Rugby League than Perpignan, the capital city of the French Catalan region. Perhaps it was the warmth of the sun reflecting brightly off the white walls of the old Brutus stadium, and the patriotic fervour of the Catalan crowd, that inspired France to get up after their 0–22 loss in Marseilles. In the event, they finished on the wrong end of a similar scoreline, but the two games were very different as Guy Laforgue and his team put in a big effort to win back pride and credibility in the second Test.

The Kiwis led 10–0 at half-time, by courtesy of two fine McGahan tries, both coming wide-out as he put the finishing touches to sweeping cross-field plays. For France, to break out of their own half and keep possession of the ball for more than two or three tackles seemed virtually impossible. They could not sustain any pressure, and the only way they were going to score a try was by some piece of French magic. And, as the game edged into its final quarter and the Catalan sun began to sink behind the grandstand, the piece of magic finally came – almost.

Winning possession from a scrum inside their own '25', France's nineteen-year-old stand-off Dominique Espugna chipped the ball ahead over the Kiwi defence. The winger, Ratier, took a good bounce and was away. The whole stadium was on its feet as Ratier used his blistering pace to arch out to the right touchline – only for Gary Kemble to come across and use every inch of his lanky frame to stretch out and cut him down with a magnificent covering tackle. But, as the winger fell to Kemble, Ratier looped the ball inside for the centre, Roger Palisses, supporting at top speed, to sprint the remaining forty yards to touch down between the posts.

It seemed as if a massive weight had been lifted from French shoulders. They had scored a try that proved they still retained their magical flair. Or so they thought. Eighty yards up at the other end of the field stood referee Ronnie Campbell, with his arm raised signifying a penalty to New Zealand. He had judged Ratier to be inches offside when he set off to chase Espugna's kick. The stands erupted in fury, and the players almost broke down and wept! To add insult to injury, referee Campbell taunted the crowd by picking up a beer-can thrown on to the pitch and pretending to drink from it – an undignified sight.

The game was over for France. Instead of being back in the contest at 6–10, with their tails up, they were back on their own line, still 10 points down, and their morale completely shot away. That 'try' would have done so much for the whole state of Rugby League in France. But, if you're offside, you're offside – sentiment doesn't enter into it.

To France's credit, they managed to keep the Kiwis at bay until the final four

6 Hugh McGahan, the Kiwis' outstanding loose forward, took over the captaincy in France when Mark Graham's serious injury forced him to return home. Against Wigan, in the Kiwis' opening game in Britain, McGahan's exciting play was affected by the torrential rain that fell throughout the match.

minutes of the game. Then Gary Kemble, who had played immaculately in both Tests, sprinted thirty-five yards to score – and, right on full-time, Kurt Sorensen backed up Friend's break to charge unopposed nearly half the length of the field to score the final try of the 1985 Kiwi tour. Olsen Filipaina's conversion provided the tour's last points, and New Zealand had secured another crushing 22–0 win, and two more World Cup points.

France: Serge Pallarès (XIII Catalan); Ratier (Lézignan), Bergé (Le Pontet), Palisses (St Estève), Couston (Le Pontet); Espugna (Lézignan), Bruno Guasch (St Estève); Chantal (Villeneuve), Bernabé (Le Pontet), Titeux (Le Pontet), Montgaillard (XIII Catalan), Palanque (Le Pontet), Guy Laforgue (XIII Catalan)

Substitutes: Andre Pérez (Toulouse) for Ratier after 71 minutes, Rabot (Villeneuve) for Chantal after 78 minutes

New Zealand: Kemble; Bell, Ah Kuoi, Leuluai, O'Hara; Filipaina, Friend; Kurt Sorensen, Wallace, Dane Sorensen, McGahan, Wright, O'Regan

Substitutes: Elia for Leuluai after 59 minutes, Todd for O'Regan after 78 minutes

Scorers: tries – McGahan (2), Kemble, Kurt Sorensen; goals – Filipaina (3)

Referee: R. Campbell (England)

Attendance: 3,045

ANGLO-FRENCH INTERNATIONALS

After their considerable achievements against New Zealand, Great Britain approached the new year, and their two Tests against France, with justified confidence. However, the two Under-21 internationals that preceded the Tests left Britain concerned at the standard of the players coming through to senior level. It was the French who surprised everybody, probably themselves included, by the quality of their play, emphasizing just how important correct coaching is to impressionable young Rugby League footballers. In previous years, the French Espoirs had appeared like no-hopers, merely aping the less endearing characteristics of their seniors, and wasting their skill and considerable athletic qualities in the process. In a very short space of time, Baitieri and Vigouroux appeared to have changed all that.

Great Britain Under-21s were stunned by their 6–19 defeat at St Estève.

Since internationals with France at Under-24 level (Great Britain dropped their age-limit to Under-21 in 1984, whilst the French Espoirs have always been, and still are, Under-23s) were re-introduced in 1976, the British had a 100 per cent record against the French. Despite the solid forward efforts of Paul Lyman, Neil Puckering and Roy Powell, the young Britons were simply out-thought and out-played at St Estève.

British observers, realizing how important to the international game in the northern hemisphere is the improvement of French playing standards, were lavish in their praise. Maurice Bamford commented: 'The young Frenchmen played an exceptionally well-organized game – their defence was very tight and they played a strong kicking game. Their discipline, too, was vastly improved on recent French teams. They never allowed our boys to set up an attacking platform.'

Outstanding for France had been their blond full-back Dumas, the scrum-half Entat, and their captain, the second-rower Montgaillard, already a full Test cap. The shock in St Estève, and the resulting media praise for Baitieri's achievements in rekindling French flair by establishing discipline, certainly added much interest to the return match played at Whitehaven two weeks later.

At St Estève the teams had been:

France Espoirs: Dumas (St Gaudens); Didier Pallarès (XIII Catalan), Lapeyre (Albi), Pougeau (Paris-Châtillon), Couston (Le Pontet); Espugna (Lézignan), Entat (Avignon); Brencz (Albi), Baco (XIII Catalan), Dorval (Paris-Châtillon), Montgaillard (XIII Catalan), Cunnac (Albi), Khedimi (St Estève)

Substitutes: Romano (Carpentras) for Cunnac after 61 minutes, Vincent Baloup (Toulouse) for Couston after 70 minutes

Scorers: tries – Dorval, Entat; goals – Dumas (5); drop goal – Dumas

Great Britain Under-21: Lyon (Widnes); Dalton (Whitehaven), Creasser (Leeds), Forster (Warrington), Carbert (Warrington); David Hulme (Widnes), Ford (Wigan); Dannatt (Hull), Puckering (Hull), Wane (Wigan), Powell (Leeds), Lyman (Featherstone Rovers), Divorty (Hull)

Substitutes: Westhead (Leigh) for Dannatt at half-time, Beckwith (Whitehaven) for Ford after 69 minutes

Scorers: try – Wane, goal – Carbert

Referee: F. Lindop (Wakefield)

Attendance: 1,820

It was an interesting, and praiseworthy, decision by the Rugby League to take the Under-21 return international to Cumbria – an area that could be described as both a stronghold and an outpost of the game in Britain. Whilst some people viewed the attendance figure of 2,539 as disappointing, presumably because over 5,000 had turned out at the same ground to watch Cumbria play the Kiwis on a pleasant autumn evening back in October, it was a far better crowd than would have been achieved for this same fixture at most grounds in Lancashire or Yorkshire. Certainly it was almost one thousand more than the local club's average home crowd, an achievement that definitely would not have been equalled elsewhere.

On a bitterly cold day, the match itself was somewhat disappointing, as once again the young Britons looked laboured as they hung on for a 6–2 win. Coach Bamford agreed, 'It was not a win to go overboard about, but rather one for spirit and determination.' Maurice was pleased that, at least, his Under-21s had got a win under their belts after three previous defeats in 1985–86 – in a trial game against Bradford Northern, against the Kiwis, and in St Estève.

Great Britain had made changes at full-back, scrum-half and hooker for the return game, and were unfortunate to lose their captain, Shaun Wane, through suspension. But, for much of the eighty minutes, the French again looked the tidier, better disciplined side, and they could feel justifiably deprived at not taking at least a draw from their efforts on this wintry afternoon. The performances of Dumas – who won the appreciation of the Whitehaven crowd not least because of his striking resemblance to their former local hero, Arnold Walker – Espugna, Entat and Baco, augured well for Tas Baitieri in his hopes of persuading the French selectors to include them in the full Test side to meet Great Britain at Avignon.

Although the Under-21s won, Great Britain could not think of promoting to Test level many of their young representatives on the strength of this performance. Only Paul Lyman made real progress in the forward battle, while Harcombe's steadiness at full-back earned him the man-of-the-match award.

Great Britain Under-21: Harcombe (Rochdale Hornets); Dalton (Whitehaven), Beckwith (Whitehaven), Forster (Warrington), Carbert (Warrington); Creasser (Leeds), David Hulme (Widnes); Powell (Leeds), Hughes (Leigh), Puckering (Hull), Divorty (Hull), Westhead (Leigh), Lyman (Featherstone Rovers)

Substitutes: Hill (Leeds) for Puckering after 60 minutes, Lyon (Widnes) not used

Scorers: try – Carbert; goal – Carbert

France Espoirs: Dumas (St Gaudens); Didier Pallarès (XIII Catalan), Lapeyre (Albi), Pougeau (Paris-Châtillon), Vincent Baloup (Toulouse); Espugna (Lézignan), Entat (Avignon); Brencz (Albi), Baco (XIII Catalan), Dorval (Paris-Châtillon), Montgaillard (XIII Catalan), Romano (Carpentras), Khedimi (St Estève)

Substitutes: Gilbert Aillères (Toulouse) for Khedimi after 60 minutes, Couston (Le Pontet) for Pougeau after 76 minutes

Scorer: goal – Dumas

Referee: J. Rascagnères (Perpignan)

Attendance: 2,539

First Test
Parc des Sports, Avignon, 16 February
France 10 Great Britain 10

The Test at Avignon was supposed to confirm Great Britain's return as a major force in international Rugby League, as well as provide two vital points in the quest for a place in the 1988 World Cup final. Instead it brought disappointment at the performance of the British team, and only one World Cup point. In the event, Great Britain were fortunate to get away with a draw at the magnificently designed Parc des Sports. The side that performed so well in the three Tests against the Kiwis – the inclusion of Henderson Gill and Shaun Wane at the expense of Joe Lydon and Andy Goodway being the only changes, in addition to the absence through injury of veteran prop Jeff Grayshon – fumbled their way through eighty minutes against France without showing any of the confident attacking play that had so rocked New Zealand.

Instead, it was left to the French to provide the exciting passages of football, as they missed chance after chance to get enough points on the board to win. Not that France were too disappointed at their failure to capitalize on their chances – a draw was far more than they really expected to take against a British side laden with brilliant individuals in the back-line, and two half-backs and a pack of forwards who had played so well against the Kiwis. France, remember, had lost both their Tests to New Zealand by resounding 0–22 margins.

7 Tony Myler, the Great Britain stand-off, is covered by France's loose forward, Thierry Bernabé, as he prepares to pass in the second Test against France at Central Park, Wigan. Britain won easily 24–10.

Great Britain's problem was that they just couldn't hang on to the ball long enough to put France under real pressure. Securing possession presented few problems as David Watkinson took the scrums 15–5 against the young Test débutant hooker Patrick Baco but the British midfield failed to stamp any authority on the game. While Britain laboured up the middle, France always seemed capable of exploding into life, with the kind of exciting running and handling that can make them so hard to come to grips with. Throughout the match, the French back three of the captain, Guy Laforgue, Marc Palanque and Thierry Bernabé were persistently dangerous, and by the final quarter were cutting the Great Britain defence to ribbons almost every time they ran with the ball. Fortunately for Britain, the French three-quarters just couldn't finish.

It was also a credit to Britain's excellent defence that they did restrict France to only one try – and especially to only two points in a first half almost completely dominated territorially by the Frenchmen.

On reflection, it was a bizarre first half. Despite winning the scrums 8–1, Great Britain hardly got out of their own half. Yet, in a few moments leading up to the interval, French promise turned to despair. A dubious penalty goal, awarded after the intrusion of a touch-judge, brought a brilliant kick from wide-out by Lee Crooks – and the French were still arguing about that penalty when they were caught sufficiently off guard for Britain finally to make a break. It was Shaun Wane who, running from midfield, burst the defence but the chance appeared to have gone when he flung a speculative inside pass that seemed well forward. However, the Australian referee, Kevin Roberts, was on the spot and was just about to put the whistle to his lips to signal the forward pass as the French defenders eased up, only for the ball to brush the arm of Max Chantal in flight, thus playing the supporting Ellery Hanley on-side. The surprised Ellery could hardly believe his good fortune as he sauntered unchallenged to the posts to touch down.

A 2–10 deficit, after dominating the half territorially, seemed too much for the French to accept as they trudged off, heads down, at half-time. They then survived a scare in the opening minutes after the re-start when Crooks sent Schofield over, only to be brought back for a forward pass. If Britain had made sure then, a 16–2 lead against an aggrieved French side feeling the whole world (or at least the whole Anglo-Saxon world) was against them, could well have paved the way to a runaway win for Maurice Bamford's men. Instead, back came the French, inspired by their excellent back three forwards, and the young half-backs, Espugna and Entat. The second half of this match at Avignon rescued Rugby League in France from the depths of despair, as Baitieri's young newcomers got themselves organized, came back, and showed that they could compete and play entertaining football at the same time.

A magical piece of initiative by Dumas split Britain's defence. He chipped ahead, took a lightning return pass from Laroche, and sprinted forty metres to the posts. Dumas, a scrum-half, now embarking on a Test career as a Paul Taylor look-alike, play-alike full-back, converted his own try to bring France up to 8–10. Into the game's final quarter, he brought the scores level with a penalty, and the very real spectre of defeat began to stare Britain in the face. As the clock ticked away, each side had opportunities to snatch victory. Dumas, incredibly, missed a drop-goal attempt from right in front of the posts, Lee Crooks saw a speculative long-distance penalty drop short, then Dumas, again, as the final act of this tense encounter, stepped up to take a penalty from a fairly inviting angle and distance. To considerable British relief, he dragged his kick wide as Kevin Roberts blew the final whistle.

So this Test ended in a 10–10 draw, against all the predictions that had made Great Britain clear favourites. Britain's disappointment was that the players who had looked so good against the Kiwis just did not reproduce that form, and made countless errors hardly expected from men of such experience and proven ability. To seriously challenge for a place in the World Cup final, Britain had banked on taking maximum points from their European neighbours. However, while Britain preferred to forget the matter as a hiccup on their road to international recovery, France continued to see some light at the end of the tunnel, under the guidance of Baitieri and Vigouroux. They included five Test débutants – Dumas, Laroche, Entat, Baco and Maury – and the step up from the Under-21 internationals was smoothly made by their youngsters, a particular point that the British management had doubted in their discussions before the event.

France: Dumas (St Gaudens); Couston (Le Pontet), Fourquet (Toulouse), Maury (Villeneuve), Laroche (Villeneuve); Espugna (Lézignan), Entat (Avignon); Chantal (Villeneuve), Baco (XIII Catalan), Titeux (Le Pontet), Guy Laforgue (XIII Catalan), Palanque (Le Pontet), Bernabé (Le Pontet)

Substitutes: Rabot (Villeneuve) for Titeux after 36 minutes, Bergé (Le Pontet) for Laroche after 77 minutes

Scorers: try – Dumas; goals – Dumas (3)

Great Britain: Burke (Widnes); Drummond (Leigh), Schofield (Hull), Hanley (Wigan), Gill (Wigan); Myler (Widnes), Fox (Featherstone Rovers); Crooks (Hull), Watkinson (Hull KR), Wane (Wigan), Potter (Wigan), Fieldhouse (Widnes), Pinner (St Helens)

Substitutes: Edwards (Wigan), James (Halifax) not used

Scorers: try – Hanley; goals – Crooks (3)

Referee: K. Roberts (Australia)

Attendance: 6,000

8 Joe Lydon, the Great Britain full-back, tries to elude the cover of his opposite number, Dumas, the young full-back from St Gaudens, in the second Britain v. France Test at Wigan.

Second Test
Central Park, Wigan, 1 March
Great Britain 24 France 10

After the disappointments of Avignon, the return Test at Wigan offered Great Britain the chance to get back on the rails. If they had had to spend the next seven months waiting for the Australians to arrive with the fortunate draw at Avignon on their minds, there would have been cause for anxiety. To Britain's credit, they made the most of their opportunity.

A confident, controlled display produced four clinically executed tries, and always kept Britain well ahead of a French team who provided firm opposition without ever looking likely to achieve victory. However, the major bonus for the British camp was the discovery of no less than four new Test players, David Laws, Tony Marchant, Neil James and Kevin Rayne. They had come into the side by default, after Pinner, Burke, Grayshon and Hanley had pulled out with injuries, but all excelled, in particular the second-rowers James and Rayne. The one significant area of weakness against the Kiwis had appeared to be the lack of attacking firepower in the British second-row. James and Rayne provided all the answers, with their strength, aggressive running and mobility. Schofield, too, was back to his brilliant best, using the ball perfectly, first for his own try, and then to provide Marchant with his first score in Test football. And up front Lee Crooks led Great Britain's pack with growing maturity.

The Wigan Test was not a World Cup qualifier, as had been the case in Avignon, and therefore did not have the same intensity. The French playing away are always a very different proposition to the French playing at home. One always had the impression, as they struggled to come to terms with the bitterly cold wind and hard pitch at Central Park, that they really hadn't even considered the possibility of victory. A respectable scoreline was the summit of France's ambitions, and they were not too disappointed when that, eventually, was how the game finished.

But, to be fair to the French, as Tas Baitieri and Vigouroux admitted afterwards, it is an enormous step up from their club competitions to Test Rugby League. They are aware of the present limitations of their players, and, bearing that in mind, they felt they had done as well as could be expected at Central Park. They had competed well enough to keep the score respectable, they had shown they could play exciting attacking football, especially when second-rower Marc Palanque ran wide, and, best of all in British eyes, they had improved their discipline immeasurably.

David Watkinson captained Great Britain for the first time in the absence of Pinner, but the main talking point, as the curtain came down on the international season, was the exciting discovery of that new second-row pairing. After the dramas of the Tests against New Zealand and in France, that was an appropriate way for Great Britain's season to end: satisfied with their progress and confident that they had some more good cards up their sleeve as the big challenge against Australia loomed in the distance.

Great Britain: Lydon (Wigan); Drummond (Leigh), Schofield (Hull), Marchant (Castleford), Laws (Hull KR); Myler (Widnes), Fox (Featherstone Rovers); Crooks (Hull), Watkinson (Hull KR), Fieldhouse (Widnes), Kevin Rayne (Leeds), James (Halifax), Potter (Wigan)

Substitutes: Platt (St Helens) for Fieldhouse after 73 minutes, Edwards (Wigan) not used

Scorers: tries – Drummond, Schofield, James, Marchant; goals – Crooks (2), Schofield (2)

France: Dumas (St Gaudens); Couston (Le Pontet), Bergé (Le Pontet), Fourquet (Toulouse), Laroche (Villeneuve); Espugna (Lézignan), Entat (Avignon); Chantal (Villeneuve), Baco (XIII Catalan), Titeux (Le Pontet), Guy Laforgue (XIII Catalan), Palanque (Le Pontet), Bernabé (Le Pontet)

Substitutes: Rabot (Villeneuve) for Chantal after 66 minutes, Serge Pallarès (XIII Catalan) for Espugna after 70 minutes

Scorers: tries – Couston (2); goal – Dumas

Referee: K. Roberts (Australia)

Attendance: 8,112

Harry Edgar

2

THE JOHN PLAYER SPECIAL TROPHY, THE JOHN SMITH'S YORKSHIRE CUP AND THE BURTONWOOD BREWERY LANCASHIRE CUP

THE JOHN PLAYER SPECIAL TROPHY

Wigan's success in winning the John Player Special Trophy was a reflection of the all-round strength developed by the Central Park club. At times they were devastating and, though occasionally looking out of sorts, they always had someone on form at the crucial stage of a match to steer them out of trouble. This was particularly the case in an epic third-round tie at Warrington and in a largely defence-dominated final against Hull Kingston Rovers. In both games Wigan had to show resilience and determination, not to mention patience.

Wigan began the competition as favourites and nothing happened on the way to the final to suggest that they would lose that tag. There was one surprise for them in the first round, however. Drawn at home to struggling second-division Mansfield, there was speculation as to whether Wigan might reach a century of points if they hit form. Perhaps that stung Mansfield into playing above themselves and made Wigan complacent for, though they won easily, a century was never on the cards.

There had been one keen preliminary tie, Warrington winning 14–10 at Featherstone in a hard game, but otherwise the round was comparatively uneventful. Castleford did not have an easy game in beating the amateurs West Hull 24–10 at the Boulevard; but Keighley won against the BARLA National Trophy holders, Jubilee, 24–6 at Lawkholme Lane and Rochdale Hornets underlined their good second division form with a 24–6 win at Carlisle.

The outstanding tie of the first round proper was at Halifax, who entertained the holders, Hull KR, in a repeat of the previous season's semi-final. Halifax were playing well, with their Australians in top form, and blending satisfactorily with the club's new British signings. Though they suffered a pre-match blow when their outstanding attacking full-back, Joe Kilroy, withdrew through injury, they still fancied their chances of revenge. The game showed what a formidable cup team Rovers had become. Halifax produced plenty of pressure but few signs of a try, while Hull KR scored two well-taken tries in the first half. One by centre Gary Prohm followed smooth handling and a slick dummy by the New Zealander, the other was a tidy piece of finishing by the winger, Garry Clark. It was a performance to make the other top clubs take notice that Rovers were not going to relinquish their trophy easily.

There was one upset, at Barrow, where struggling Leeds were outplayed. Barrow's try, by Andy Whittle, was modest reward for almost total domination, belied by the slender 5–2 score. Some first-division sides were stretched before winning through against teams from the lower region. Widnes were taken all the way at Whitehaven, where tries by Basnett and Cleal and two goals by Barry Dowd enabled them to scrape home 12–7 after some desperate late moments. Warrington had to work hard at Fulham, Mark Forster touching down twice in a 20–13 win and Salford just edged out Rochdale Hornets 18–12. Leigh took their rampaging league form into the competition with a 70–2 win at Batley, the often underrated winger Phil Fox scoring five tries and John Henderson three.

York have developed a habit of beating Castleford at Wigginton Road, so their 12–10 win was not a complete surprise. Graham Steadman landed four goals for the home team and they were saved when Castleford's Ian French lost the ball when over the try-line. Overall there was the feeling that the first round had been just a little flat.

The highlight of the second round was an excellent contest at Craven Park where Hull KR were slightly fortunate to pip an Oldham side unbeaten in their previous nine games. Oldham had their full-back David Liddiard sent off after thirty minutes, when they trailed 3–6, but they raised their game and twenty minutes from the end, with Rovers ahead 8–3, Oldham were awarded a penalty in front of the posts. It seemed an easy two points, but their scrum-half, Ray Ashton, tried a quick tap in a bid for a try and the chance was lost. The importance of this miss was stressed when Warnecke's break and kick-ahead brought a try for Hussein M'Barki to narrow the gap to a point but David Hobbs was unable to land what would have been the match-winning goal.

There was a fascinating performance at St Helens by no-hopers Doncaster. Their emergence as a useful second-division side had passed unnoticed but when their prop, Kevin Parkhouse, plunged over to put them 12–10 ahead in the second half, Knowsley Road was stunned. The prospect of dead bodies all over the East Lancashire Road was removed by a late Saints' flourish, led by Neil Holding, to take them to a 36–20 win but the Dons had earned respectability and were to add to it later in the season.

There was a time when a Wakefield Trinity *v.* Wigan game would have been the match of any round but Trinity are a more modest outfit these days as their second-division status indicates. It was a match which emphasized how Wigan can ease through the gears when required. They led only 16–13 at the interval but a quick burst took them clear at 30–13 until Trinity restored pride with two late tries, to finish 21–30.

Barrow's giant killing ended tamely at Warrington, 14–34, while Leigh disappointed their fans by beating Hunslet only 48–6 at Hilton Park – they had hoped for fifty points – with Henderson scoring three more tries. Scrum-half Andy Gascoigne, Hull's bargain buy from Bramley, nipped in for two tries in their 30–10 win over Salford at the Boulevard, while York had to struggle to hold off a spirited Keighley challenge, winning 21–16 as Mick Hawksworth scored two tries for the visitors. Widnes outplayed Bradford Northern, in the televised fixture, but it took a fine try by Cleal, his second of the match, to spur them to a late rush of points that brought a 30–6 victory.

The third round brought two breathtaking matches, at Warrington and Widnes. The Warrington tie showed Wigan's mettle as a side of all-round ability and character. They were shaken by a blistering Warrington opening in which Tom Gittins stayed upright in a tackle to send Paul Bishop darting over, Bishop adding the goal himself. Wigan steadied when Steve Ella sent Henderson Gill in at the corner, but a mighty break by Les Boyd, from Gregory's shrewd pass, sent Blake to the posts and Bishop's second goal made it 12–4. This really was a test for Wigan and they scored an important try just before the interval through Ellery Hanley, and David Stephenson's goal put them within range. Wigan looked an imposing team early in the second half. A try by Ella, following his own kick, and a typical weaving effort from Gill put them in charge but a Bishop goal narrowed the score to 14–18. Then Ian Potter scored a remarkable try as Warrington's defence hesitated, were punished for a couple of sloppy tackles and Wigan apparently were in control again at 24–14. But a sparkling long-range try by Rick Thackray and two goals by Bishop again opened things up for Warrington before Stephenson calmed matters with a late penalty. The match, with the final score 26–22 to Wigan, had been a credit to both sides.

Memorable, too, was the tie at Widnes, where Leigh's Des Drummond was in marvellous form as his side ran out winners by 35–31. Drummond's contribution was a hat-trick of tries, including one dazzling run the length of the field, after Widnes had stormed ahead 12–0 in the first five minutes. Leigh fought back to level the score at 18–18 by the interval. Then Widnes lost their prop, Mike O'Neill, sent off in the second half as they fought to hold the second-division leaders, and Drummond's tries settled the tie after a great struggle.

York showed plenty of enterprise in going close against Hull KR, where they trailed only 16–18 with five minutes left, hooker Peter Phillippo scoring two of their tries. Inevitably it was Gavin Miller who clinched things for Rovers with a late try, but the kicking of John Dorahy was vital as he landed six goals.

The St Helens tie against Hull at Knowsley Road was delayed because the visitors had their Kiwi stars on Test duty in France. However, it was worth the wait for Saints, who, after their second-round struggle against Doncaster, took Hull apart to gain an astonishing 57–14 win. Paul Forber scored three tries and there were two each for Conlon, Ledger and Holding.

The semi-final draw brought the prospect of a Wigan *v.* Hull KR final, which most enthusiasts were probably hoping for. Wigan first had to meet the challenge of a Leigh side who had piled up 153 points in their three previous ties, while Hull KR were again at Headingley for a semi-final, this time against St Helens.

It was a measure of Wigan's stature that though they were thought to have played below form against Leigh at Knowsley Road, they had nevertheless registered a record score for a semi-final in winning 36–8 against a team very much on form. Certainly it seemed that Wigan were sometimes a shade lucky with the bounce of the ball and few of their tries stemmed from the sort of flashing attacking play for which they were noted. Yet the comfortable way they handled Leigh in the last half-hour with only twelve men, following the dismissal of Colin Whitfield, spoke volumes for their quality. When Whitfield was sent off, Wigan led 18–8, and there was the possibility of a desperate finish. The threat never materialized. Wigan reorganized so effectively that Leigh were completely subdued and Wigan registered 18 more points without reply.

The match was a personal triumph for the Wigan prop, Greg Dowling, a marvellously efficient front-row man. He came from Australia with a fiery and outspoken reputation but he let his rugby do the talking and had an exemplary record throughout the season. His hat-trick of tries against Leigh came from being in the right place at the right time and he also showed an ability to move the ball well. It was Dowling's pass that ricocheted from the unlucky Tony Cottrell to give Ella the first Wigan try after an energetic Leigh opening had been thwarted. Ella then returned the compliment, sending Dowling in for the first of his tries and Wigan were on their way.

Wigan were coasting, perhaps too easily, just after the half-hour, when the Leigh scrum-half, Phil Johnson, caught them napping and scored a good solo try, Chris Johnson failing with an easy kick that would have put Leigh in touch. Before the interval Wigan struck again when Stephenson's high kick bounced off Chris Johnson and Dowling plunged over for his second try.

An interval lead of 18–4 looked more than enough for Wigan but they were hit early in the second half by a spectacular score. Pyke, Westhead and Henson all handled in fine style to get Fox into his stride. The winger still had plenty to do but took his chance well for the best try of the match. Then Leigh's hopes were raised higher still by the dismissal of Whitfield. However, Wigan again fought back to take control. Good play by Wane and Kiss sent Hanley over and Kiss himself crossed before Dowling collected his third try. Stephenson took his goal tally to six, again a semi-final record, and Wigan sat back to see who their opponents in the final would be.

Hull KR's 22–4 win over St Helens was in some ways similar to Wigan's triumph, with Rovers very much in charge but without really setting the stands alight. A cold, wet and windy day and a poor crowd of only 3,751 set the tone for the afternoon and the match never reached the heights. Saints were very much the underdogs when the absence through injury of Harry Pinner was made public but they were given the early encouragement of a good penalty goal by Conlon.

Rovers, however, have become a very fine cup team, well-organized and thoroughly professional in their big-match approach. Once they were ahead, St Helens never really threatened to break the Rovers' stranglehold, despite brave flurries by Roy Haggerty and nimble work from Holding. The injury to that hard-working prop Tony Burke after only thirteen minutes was another blow for St Helens and they were steadily driven back as Rovers turned the screw. Yet the first Hull KR try was something of a bonus, for it came after a penalty miss by Dorahy. Brett French, seeking to take the ball near his line from Dorahy's kick, fatally knocked-on, giving Rovers the advantage at a scrum just a few yards out. David Watkinson duly won the heel and Harkin's pass sent Miller almost strolling over. This time Dorahy added the goal.

Miller's well-judged passes frequently brought the best out of prop Peter Johnston, who made a lot of ground, and Rovers continued to dominate. They opened out to give Clark a half-chance; he looked well covered but slipped and swayed past three defenders to score a good try from his point of view but one that raised questions about the Saints' cover.

With a 10–4 interval lead Rovers clearly felt that only their own mistakes would let St Helens in. Rovers proceeded to keep their opponents comfortably in check without really threatening themselves and it was not until the closing minutes that they rounded things off. French was again out of luck when he lost possession on his own '25'. Prohm gathered and quickly sent Phil Hogan over. With two minutes left Rovers added the icing when Miller and Hogan moved smartly to send Mike Smith over unopposed. Dorahy's goals inflated the margin but there was no doubting Rovers' right to be in the final again.

John Player Special Trophy Final
Elland Road, Leeds, 11 January
Wigan 11 Hull KR 8

In prospect, Hull KR *v.* Wigan was a popular final; they were two sides of proven ability and were full of star names. It may have been that expectations were too great, however. Though the game was thoroughly enjoyed by the connoisseur – after all, strong tackling is an important part of the game – some neutrals were less enthusiastic.

Rovers had their pre-match problems. Injuries ruled out their full-back, George Fairbairn, and their second-row forward, Phil Hogan, but their most important absentee was their centre, Gary Prohm. He was a victim of the icy weather as postponed games prevented him clearing before the final the second match of a two-match suspension. His lethal finishing was sadly missed. However, Rovers issued a declaration of intent when they named the sturdy Gordon Smith at stand-off, clearly to keep an eye on the dangerous Ella, and switched their try-poacher, Mike Smith, to centre.

Wigan had their former Springbok Rugby Union wing star, Ray Mordt, playing only his second game of Rugby League and were generally at full strength. It was soon clear that quick and hard tackling was to be the order of the day with both sides reluctant and often unable to take risks with their handling. Perhaps it needed Rovers to break a few points clear and make Wigan come out of their shell but Hull KR, although leading briefly in the second half by a point, never had that luxury. However, they had the game's outstanding player in Paul Harkin and John Lydiat had an excellent game in Fairbairn's place.

There were times when Wigan's Mike Ford looked in vain for forwards to come on to his passes in planned moves and their best man was not a big name but the talented youngster Shaun Wane. When they took the lead after twelve minutes it was from a considerable rarity, a left-foot drop goal by Dowling, which, he admitted later, was only the second of his career, the other coming in a cup final in Australia, which shows his sense of timing. Wigan certainly looked the more adventurous side but were rocked when a sharp pass from

9 Ellery Hanley, the Wigan centre, shows spectacular style as he leaps clear of an attempted tackle by Hull KR's Mike Smith, but then faces the formidable Gavin Miller in the final of the John Player Trophy. Wigan won 11–8.

Miller set Johnston moving and a promising raid only broke down when Gordon Smith was unable to hold the latter's pass.

Wigan gave Mordt a run and he soon felt the quality of RL tackling when he ran hard and straight into a no-nonsense cover. Wigan went deep, however, and after twenty-eight minutes scored the first try. It was slightly unexpected as Rovers, pinned close to their line, held off the sixth tackle, expecting the traditional kick for the line. Wane had other ideas, however, and drove straight over from acting half-back to give Stephenson an easy goal. At 7–0 Wigan had daylight between themselves and Rovers.

Hull KR came back with a splendid move involving Harkin, Kelly, Gordon Smith and Laws and, just on half-time, struck an important blow. They won a scrum inside the Wigan '25'. Harkin went blind and judged his pass perfectly to send the eager Lydiat in at the corner to cut the arrears to three points. Wigan resumed with Nicky Du Toit in place of Potter and a need to assert their authority. However, there were occasions when Ford went for planned moves but found no forward coming on to the ball as Rovers tackled with rare fervour. Then Johnston was held just short from Miller's pass and Wane went close at the other end before Dowling lost possession.

Rovers came out of defence in style and Lydiat tore through, again from a pass from Miller, before he was stopped by a good tackle from Ford. Then a long pass from Dorahy sent Laws over for another quality try and Rovers led 8–7. To their great credit Wigan stirred themselves and played their best rugby of the match in the next few minutes, refusing to give Rovers time to dwell on their lead. Hanley went on a run, supported by Goodway, and Du Toit was stopped just short. With the Rovers defence stretched, the ball was moved swiftly across the line and Ford went in unopposed at the corner with two men in support – a fine example of top-class rugby.

The last twenty minutes were enthralling with Rovers always menacing and Wigan trying desperately to stretch their lead. Dorahy failed with a reasonable penalty shot and with five minutes left Burton was sent off for a clumsy foul on Wane. Even then Rovers had the better of the dying minutes but failed to snatch the vital score. Afterwards, their coach, Roger Millward, said he couldn't fault his team for effort and had high praise for the man-of-the-match Paul Harkin.

Wigan: Hampson; Mordt, Stephenson, Hanley, Gill; Ella, Ford; Dowling, Kiss, Wane, West, Goodway, Potter

Substitutes: Du Toit for Potter at half-time, Edwards for Gill after 74 minutes

Scorers: tries – Wane, Ford; goal – Stephenson; drop goal – Dowling

Hull KR: Lydiat; Clark, Mike Smith, Dorahy, Laws; Gordon Smith, Harkin; Johnston, Watkinson, Ema, Burton, Kelly, Miller

Substitutes: Robinson for Johnston after 74 minutes, Rudd not used

Scorers: tries – Lydiat, Laws

Referee: J. Holdsworth (Kippax)

Attendance: 17,573

Trevor Watson

THE JOHN SMITH'S YORKSHIRE CUP

Hull Kingston Rovers gave their coach, Roger Millward, an early-season present when they won the John Smith's Yorkshire Cup. It was the first time they had collected the cup since Millward took over as coach in 1977, completing for him a full set of major competition trophies. During a period of great success for Rovers they felt frustrated at failing to win for no less than eleven years the 'easiest' tournament of them all. The frustration was the more acute because the Yorkshire Cup remained across the city in the Boulevard boardroom for a record three successive years, culminating with a victory over Rovers in the previous year's final. So Hull KR felt their 1985–86 triumph to be overdue, though they had to survive a frantic last fifteen minutes in the final against Castleford at Headingley which, for their followers, must have seemed to last all of eleven years. Castleford pulled back from 6–22 to 18–22 and tried desperately for the extra score to end their run as perennial bridesmaids, having suffered so much in semi-finals and finals against one or other of the Hull clubs. They failed and Rovers' long wait was rewarded.

Many at Craven Park were convinced the trophy was on its way after the first round in which they edged out their Boulevard neighbours in a tense and exciting affair, with Hull coming close to victory. Lee Crooks was in magnificent form for Hull and he set up the first try for Dane O'Hara. Rovers fretted when Chris Burton lost the ball over the line but drew level just before the interval when Hogan dummied his way over. Lee Crooks struck again, this time supporting a move by Ah Kuoi and Leuluai to score, and Divorty's goal pushed Hull 10–4 ahead. A penalty by Dorahy narrowed the gap but Hull hung on until seven minutes from the end, when Hogan went in for his second try. Dorahy's goal had one half of Humberside celebrating. A good sign for Rovers was a fine performance by the teenage prop, Des Harrison.

Elsewhere there were some strange matches, not least at Headingley. The second-division strugglers Keighley forged 12–4 ahead against Leeds and were 12–10 up at the break. Their game then fell apart in the second half, Leeds scoring fifty points without reply, with the Australian Cliff Lyons scoring three tries. There was also a spectacular long-range try for a Welsh trialist winger. He proved to be Steve Ford, shortly to gain some notoriety. Ford decided to sign for Leeds, but then changed his mind, only to find himself banned for life by the Welsh Rugby Union because he had effectively turned professional during his trial period at Headingley. The dispute that followed rumbled on throughout the season.

10 Barry Johnson, the Castleford prop, tries to struggle clear of the Hull KR defence in the Yorkshire Cup final and still has to overcome Hull KR's covering loose forward, Gavin Miller. Miller played a great game in Rovers' 22–18 victory.

Another second-division club, Wakefield Trinity, were 9–4 ahead in the second half against Bradford Northern at Odsal. The dismissal of their player-coach, Len Casey, against his old club was too big a blow for Wakefield, however, and they too collapsed in the second half, going down 15–40. Stand-off Graham Steadman scored all of York's eighteen points against Featherstone Rovers only to finish on the losing side. Here again a sending-off proved crucial. York lost Peter Phillippo, did not win a scrum from that point and Rovers went through 26–18. Winger Chris Chapman and centre Tony Marchant scored four tries each as Castleford won against Hunslet by the huge margin of 60–2. Bramley beat Doncaster 22–10 and Dewsbury upheld first-division dignity with a hard-earned 14–10 win over Batley at Mount Pleasant.

Leeds continued their high scoring in the second round, thrashing Dewsbury 48–2 at Crown Flatt, a record score at this venue for the Headingley men. Hull

KR were never in trouble at home to Bramley but two late tries by Gary Prohm inflated their margin over spirited opponents to 30–6. Castleford had their second-row forward, Keith England, sent off in the first half at Halifax but still had too much pace and power for a side yet to feel the benefit of their Australian signings and won comfortably 24–4. Featherstone Rovers held an 11–4 advantage over Bradford Northern. That is usually enough at Post Office Road but Northern's Dean Carroll and John Woods turned things upside down, Carroll scoring twice as Bradford won 22–11.

It was a pity that the pressure of the New Zealand tour meant that the Yorkshire and Lancashire semi-finals had to be played on the same night. The 10,334 who chose Leeds against Castleford saw a splendid contest. Castleford's John Joyner was outstanding at loose forward and there was penetrating running from a little-known second-row forward, Martin Ketteridge. Joyner's classic break and well-timed pass enabled Tony Spears to race in for the first try, goaled by Bob Beardmore, to give Castleford an interval lead. Leeds came back strongly in the second half and a gem of a pass by Lyons sent Mark Wilson in for a good try. Creasser's touchline goal levelled matters. Leeds went ahead when Heron and Maskill inter-passed and the latter swerved clear to send winger Andy Smith over. Another Heron break should have produced a try before Castleford countered in style, creating a try for their winger, David Plange, to make it 10–10. The way both teams were attacking meant that a draw was never on the cards. At length the winning score came when Joyner was half-held in the tackle but kept the ball alive to send the full-back, David Roockley, through. He kicked for the corner and Spears dived for the touchdown to take Castleford into the final.

Hull KR were firm favourites against Bradford Northern, who played with rare spirit. Two penalties by Dorahy put Rovers on the right path but they were shaken by the effort of the Northern forwards and the visitors went ahead through two goals and a drop goal by John Woods. After thirty-three minutes Burton's break gave Prohm the chance to show his finishing skills again and he beat two defenders for a good try. It proved the only try of the game, though Northern had a 'score' disallowed when Wayne Heron crossed the line only for the pass to be ruled forward, and there was the possibility of a score from a thrilling run from Richard Francis. Rovers were glad of a goal by Dorahy to complete a hard-earned 11–5 win.

The Yorkshire Cup Final
Headingley, Leeds, October 27
Hull KR 22 Castleford 18

With a Sunday date and no television, RL's armchair followers missed an enthralling game with a cliffhanger finish, some sparkling tries and a virtuoso performance at loose forward by Rovers' Gavin Miller. When the teams were announced it was seen that Castleford had preferred Gary Lord at full-back to Roockley while Rovers were without Mike Smith and had Gordon Smith at stand-off.

Rovers went ahead with a penalty by Dorahy after eight minutes. They looked the more imaginative side and seven minutes later produced a quality try. Their New Zealanders, Smith and Prohm, made the running and the Australian Gavin Miller was on the spot to score. Dorahy's goal made it 8–0. Castleford were struggling to make a clean break but one came when Barry Johnson sent Bob Beardmore into space. When challenged, Beardmore kicked ahead and the ball rolled enticingly over the line. Garry Clark was there first but he failed to make it safe and Beardmore dived for the touchdown. Surprisingly he missed the easy goal-kick and Dorahy nudged Rovers 10–4 ahead with his third goal before Diamond landed a penalty for Castleford just on the interval.

The second half bristled with good rugby. Rovers took a firm grip with two tries in the space of seven minutes and Miller was involved in both. First, he sold a prodigious dummy and sailed clear to score himself, Dorahy adding the goal. Then he drove hard up the right-hand touchline. The ground gained was creditable enough but Miller then produced a perfect pass from a three-man tackle to give Clark a clear run to the line. It was a masterly piece of play and Dorahy added a touchline goal, his fifth and a record for the Yorkshire final. Castleford were in danger of being over-run at this stage but Kevin Ward had other ideas. He began to use his strength to great purpose and launched a revival. Marchant had one 'try' disallowed before Ward charged for the line and his slick pass sent Marchant over, Bob Beardmore adding the goal. Now it was 22–12 to Rovers with fifteen minutes left.

With eight minutes to go Ward surged forward again. As he tried to slip out a pass near the line the ball bounced free, Rovers failed to cover and Marchant plunged for his second try. Bob Beardmore's goal made only four points in it. Castleford stretched Rovers in those frantic closing minutes but Rovers held out and Millward had completed his trophy collection.

Hull KR: Fairbairn; Clark, Dorahy, Prohm, Laws; Gordon Smith, Harkin; Harrison, Watkinson, Ema, Burton, Hogan, Miller

Substitutes: Lydiat for Fairbairn at half-time, Kelly for Hogan after 73 minutes.

Scorers: tries – Miller (2), Clark; goals – Dorahy (5)

Castleford: Lord; Spears, Marchant, Hyde, Plange; Diamond, Bob Beardmore; Ward, Kevin Beardmore, Johnson, England, Ketteridge, Joyner

Substitutes: Roockley and Horton not used

Scorers: tries – Marchant (2), Bob Beardmore; goals – Bob Beardmore (2), Diamond

Referee: R. Campbell (Widnes)

Attendance: 12,686

Trevor Watson

THE BURTONWOOD BREWERY LANCASHIRE CUP

Though unaccustomed to being second best to anybody, Wigan were anything but blasé about their prospects of winning the Lancashire Cup. Now the heady delights of the previous May's Wembley final were only a memory to set against the blunt realities of a new season. Henderson Gill, one of their great individualists on the left wing, had broken his ankle in the opening match of the season and they had lost their first three league matches when the county cup competition began. They were firmly at the bottom of the first-division table.

Even their first round tie against second-division Fulham must have caused their supporters grave anxiety. Fulham were leading 13–12 only ten minutes from time when Wigan's latest and highly expensive forward signing, Andrew Goodway, the former Oldham international, prised open a gap in a stubborn defence. Timing his pass perfectly, Goodway sent his wing, Phil Ford, squeezing in at the corner. Ironically, Ford was part of the bait Wigan were using to tempt Bradford Northern to part with Ellery Hanley. Ford's try ended any hopes Fulham had of producing a shock result at Central Park and Wigan won 24–13, which looked a more comfortable margin than it was.

The first round brought no surprises, though Oldham must have wondered why the competition was becoming an all-too-familiar disaster area for them. After suffering unexpected defeats in the previous two seasons, they slumped again, horrifically, against second-division Leigh at Hilton Park. John Henderson, who was to prove one of the most promising centres of the season, scored two tries in Leigh's 40–12 triumph. Rochdale Hornets, newly revived after a close season boardroom take-over, gave Widnes a hard match before losing 6–17.

The local derby between Salford and Swinton produced one of the hardest fought ties of the round. Salford were leading 9–8 when Paul Groves, the Under-21 international hooker, was sent off for a high tackle in the forty-ninth minute, five minutes after the Swinton captain, Alan Hodkinson, who was to retire in a few weeks, had been banished to the sin-bin for ten minutes for dissent. Salford survived to win 18–14, thanks largely to an inspiring try by John Pendlebury, their captain and loose forward. In another local derby, in Cumbria this time, Barrow were knocked out at Craven Park by Whitehaven's solid tackling and lively attack. But it was a close run thing before Whitehaven won 12–8.

Like Pliny's Africa, there always seems to be something new out of Wigan. Not content with introducing the glamorous Hanley to the Lancashire Cup, they also fielded a mystery trialist at right centre in their second-round tie against Salford at Central Park. Although they were too polite to say so, Wigan expected a reasonably relaxed stroll through that tie. And so it seemed when they led 18–2 at half-time and 22–2 after forty-nine minutes. What followed was to produce one of the most enthralling finishes of the competition.

The first half followed the expected pattern: Wigan were confident, assured and impressive on attack while Salford battled gamely to contain them. After only one minute the trialist kicked a penalty when Gary Disley, Salford's boisterous open-side prop, was punished for holding down Shaun Wane after a tackle. In the fourteenth minute, Hanley and the scrum-half, Mike Ford, opened up a gap and Ford's neat inside pass gave Goodway the chance to go over for the first try, with the trialist, a more than useful kicker, adding the goal. Wigan supporters, forming the bulk of the 11,188 crowd, had the moment they wanted when Hanley produced the sort of try that has made him the most expensive player in British Rugby League. Setting off on a diagonal run from half-way, Hanley showed his speed and strength in brushing off two would-be tacklers to score.

Seven minutes later, Goodway and Hanley opened the way for Steve Hampson, who had a splendid match at full-back, to score and again the trialist kicked the goal. Shortly before half-time, Wane was penalized for obstruction and Griffiths's goal gave Salford their first points. Salford's few first-half attacks proved no more than a minor irritant but early in the second half came the first hint that they had something more to offer. It came from a long break by Paul Groves. He raced through a broken field but fell to a solid tackle by Hampson. Four minutes later Neil Baker, a master of the short kick-and-gather, broke away only to see the ball roll dead.

Wigan slapped down these moments of Salford cheekiness with a dazzling try, started by stand-off Shaun Edwards and carried on by the second-row forward Nicky Du Toit, left wing Jimmy Fairhurst, the trialist and finishing with a try from the New Zealand right wing, Gary Henley-Smith. Henley-Smith retired injured a minute later, with Du Toit moving to the centre, the trialist to the right wing and Neil Courtney, the substitute, joining the pack. With only twenty minutes left the result seemed a formality. Instead, Salford rallied magnificently, catching Wigan in a swathe of complacency. It began innocently enough in the sixty-sixth minute when the Australian centre, Mike Pobjie, sent Baker in at the corner with Griffiths kicking an excellent goal.

It was Baker who was to dominate the remainder of the match with his marvellous distribution and clever tactical kicking. Baker had a notable ally in scrum-half Darren Bloor, unusually tall for the position, but a player with fire and determination. From a scrum, the loose forward, John Pendlebury, deceived the Wigan defence and slipped out a pass that sent Bloor on an unstoppable scoring run. With seven minutes left, Salford were trailing only 14–22 and two minutes from time Bloor set up the move that was finished by the right wing, Ian Marsh. Griffiths kicked his fourth goal and Wigan barely managed to hang on until the final whistle. There were more signs of celebration in Salford's dressing-room than in Wigan's where the mood was one of relief. 'We were all over them – we ran out of time,' claimed the Salford manager, Kevin Ashcroft. Who would argue with him? Certainly not Wigan!

There was just as much excitement at near-by Leigh, who led 14–12 at half-time against Widnes. In fact, Widnes looked shattered when Leigh quickly ran up fourteen points through tries from Phil Fox and John Kerr, and two goals and a penalty from Phil Johnson. Widnes gradually regained their poise, helped by tries from John Myler and David Lamb, both improved by Joe Lydon. Leigh never crumpled under pressure but were beaten by a well-taken try by half-back David Hulme with John Myler adding the goal.

The other ties went according to plan. Warrington's 38–4 win over Workington was memorable for the debut of Phil Blake, just arrived from Sydney, who showed his pace and class in scoring two tries. St Helens, the holders, had an easy 26–8 win over Whitehaven. They missed the injured Harry Pinner at loose forward and even more the giant centre Mal Meninga, who had not returned from Australia to repeat his match-winning feats of last season.

Never was Meninga's absence more apparent than in St Helens's semi-final against Wigan. Saints held out until the last three minutes of the first half when the prop-forward, Shaun Wane, and the stand-off, Shaun Edwards, scored tries, and a goal from Stephenson gave Wigan a 10–0 half-time lead. Midway through the second half the Australian Test stand-off Steve Ella, who had flown in from Sydney only twelve hours earlier, came on as substitute and scored the last try of the match in Wigan's 30–2 victory, a result and a performance by Saints that must have made the previous season's triumph in the final seem a long way away.

Warrington had a harder time beating Widnes 11–4 in the other semi-final and again it was Blake, playing in the centre, who stood out. Another Australian, the controversial prop-forward Les Boyd, made his début. Considering it was his first match for fifteen months after being suspended in Sydney he lasted surprisingly well.

The Lancashire Cup Final
Knowsley Road, St Helens, 13 October
Wigan 34 Warrington 8

The final, played at Knowsley Road, St Helens, was something of an anti-climax. This was due mainly to an ill-disciplined display by Warrington, who had their loose forward, Alan Rathbone, and their scrum-half, Andy Gregory, sent off in the second half. Rathbone was dismissed in the fifty-fourth minute for a late tackle on Wigan's loose forward, Ian Potter, and eight minutes from time Gregory followed for stamping on Du Toit. The pity of it was that Warrington were good value in the first half and led 8–2 after twenty-two minutes.

Stephenson opened the scoring with a second-minute penalty, followed by one by the Warrington wing, Brian Carbert, six minutes later. Warrington were unlucky to lose Blake, so important to their attack, through injury after twenty-seven minutes. Earlier they had scored an exciting try when Gregory broke on the blind-side and their full-back, Brian Johnson, another talented Australian, took his pass to race seventy yards to score. Carbert added the goal with an in-off shot. Wigan, however, began to play more steadily, and had looked threatening before hooker Nicky Kiss ploughed over for a try after thirty minutes.

11 The outstanding skill of Greg Dowling, Wigan's Australian prop, was an important factor in Wigan's Lancashire Cup success. In the final they crushed Warrington 34–8.

Almost on half-time Ella scored a breathtaking try, arrogant in its execution. Confronted by a solid barrier of defenders he sold two thrilling dummies and then changed direction to bluff his opponents completely. Stephenson's goal sent Wigan in at half-time leading 12–8. He added a penalty after nine minutes of the second half and Rathbone departed five minutes later. This as good as finished Warrington for within three minutes Ella raced away for his second try, cutting inside the left wing, Rick Thackray, to score. Two penalties from Stephenson and tries from Hanley and Edwards, both improved by Stephenson, produced the highest-ever score of 34–8 in the final, beating St Helens's 30–2 defeat of Oldham in 1968. Wigan are the unchallenged pacesetters of the Lancashire Cup competition with a record thirty-one final appearances and a total of seventeen wins. Sadly, the match on a sunny afternoon signalled the end of the Burtonwood Brewery's sponsorship.

Wigan: Edwards; Henley-Smith, Stephenson, Hanley, Whitfield; Ella, Ford; Dowling, Kiss, Wane, Du Toit, Goodway, Potter

Substitutes: Case for Wane after 27 minutes, Hampson for Henley-Smith after 58 minutes

Scorers: tries – Kiss, Ella (2), Hanley, Edwards; goals – Stephenson (7)

Warrington: Johnson; Carbert, Cullen, Blake, Thackray; Kelly, Andy Gregory; Eccles, Webb, Jackson, Boyd, Mike Gregory, Rathbone

Substitutes: Forster for Blake after 27 minutes, Kevin Tamati for Boyd after 48 minutes, Boyd for Eccles after 63 minutes, Eccles for Mike Gregory after 66 minutes

Scorers: try – Johnson; goals – Carbert (2)

Referee: J. Holdsworth (Kippax)

Attendance: 19,202

Jack McNamara

3

THE SILK CUT CHALLENGE CUP

Whatever else happens during a nine-month Rugby League season, there is one event that is guaranteed to rouse passions and spark arguments all through the summer. The annual struggle to reach Wembley and take home the Challenge Cup is the greatest of all battles in the hard-headed world of the professional rugby player.

In 1986, the competition's second year under the Silk Cut promotional banner, with a British winter at its worst, the Cup needed all its traditional appeal to get off the ground, especially in the early rounds. For the first time in four years, to the delight of most fans of Rugby League, two leading amateur clubs were welcomed back. Three amateur teams went into the preliminary round bag at Headingley but one was to be discarded before the contest proper was allowed to get under way. Simms Cross from Widnes were paired to meet Dudley Hill of Bradford in a qualifier, and as early as that the weather started to play havoc. The two teams made four attempts to get the game played at Bramley's McLaren Field before they eventually overcame the frost, Dudley Hill beating Simms Cross to earn a draw away to Hull on Humberside.

The other amateurs in the eight-team preliminary round were the champions of Cumbria, Kells. They were due to visit Hunslet at Elland Road, one venue where the weather could not interfere because of the undersoil heating, and a crowd of 1,200 might have shivered to death but for some heart-warming efforts from the amateurs. Kells were beaten 8–20 but they did the amateur game proud and the Hunslet chairman, Gerry Mason, was a relieved man when he paid tribute to his beaten opponents afterwards. And he had no complaints about the Silk Cut award of £75 for the outstanding player of the match going to Kells's loose forward, Paul Messenger. (It needs to be hastily added that the cheque was made payable to the club and Paul retained his amateur status!)

On Humberside, Dudley Hill lived up to their responsibilities as ambassadors for the amateur game when a crowd of 2,590 turned up to see them take on Hull. A 38–10 victory for the previous year's finalists reflected the size of the task that Dudley Hill had taken on but, like Kells, they did not leave empty-handed. Gary Brentley won the player-of-the-match award.

Unfortunately for the professionals, the other two preliminary-round games passed almost unnoticed. Leeds's comfortable victory over Swinton at Station Road was largely unmemorable, while Carlisle's 20–14 win over Mansfield Marksman brought little extra attention to either club.

Then the weather grew even worse; wholesale postponements caused headaches all round and more than one or two arguments as the Cup almost went into cold storage. To make matters worse, Humberside got the one match it did not want – Hull Kingston Rovers *v.* Hull FC. 'We would rather have saved them for Wembley,' said a philosophical Hull chairman, Roy Waudby, when the draw was made. (At that time he acknowledged that they still had Dudley Hill to overcome!) And there was a certain amount of sympathy for both Hull clubs from all neutral RL supporters though not from the clubs with their own Wembley ambitions. They knew that at least one of the main challengers would drop by the wayside.

Not unnaturally this game was chosen as the live televised fixture and, astonishingly for RL-mad Humberside, the gate dipped to 8,770. John Dorahy – Joe Cool to his huge band of supporters both in Britain and in Australia – was the match-winner for Rovers. His five goals and the three tries from his fellow Australian Gavin Miller, Andy Kelly and Mike Smith eased Rovers into the second round by 22–6.

As the other matches eventually sorted themselves out a new set of unlikely heroes arose. Doncaster, cannon fodder for years, suddenly found their own ammunition, and poor old Salford suffered. On a Tatters Field mudheap, the one-time glamour boys from Manchester were given an 18–12 beating and suddenly Doncaster were no longer simply 'that team who were in *Another Bloody Sunday*'.

Blackpool, too, made a little bit of history. They passed the first hurdle for the first time in twenty-one years, though their 30–10 victory over Runcorn was hardly in the same category of giant-killing as Doncaster's. Oldham, Warrington, Castleford and Wigan all topped a half-century of points but the first round of the Challenge Cup was not all sweetness and light.

Dewsbury, for instance, were on the brink of pulling out altogether. Frost and ice and more frost prevented their game against St Helens and Alex Murphy from going ahead – not once, not twice, but half a dozen times. They were told to switch the game to heated Headingley. 'You can't make us,' they claimed. 'The weather isn't our fault.' And so the wrangle went on until, with the deadline fast approaching, Dewsbury, later to be relegated, agreed. But in the end, they may have had a point about losing ground advantage. Fewer than 2,000 turned up at Leeds and, despite their most stirring performance of the season, Dewsbury lost. As the winter refused to relax its icy grip, they were not the only sufferers. Dates were juggled until a whole draw was put off because of the uncertainties of the weather. Undersoil heating was on constantly at Wigan and Leeds. Bradford, frozen out of Odsal, played Wakefield Trinity at Leeds in their first-round tie on the day the second round should have been in full swing. They survived the move, winning 10–8 in front of the TV cameras.

Fulham, already on the brink of collapse and in desperate need of a Cup run to boost their flagging fortunes, had an attractive home draw in promotion-candidates Barrow. Unfortunately, the faithful of Chiswick had to travel north to Wigan on a bleak midwinter's night to see their heroes lose 14–26. It was the beginning of the end for Roy Close-inspired Fulham. Soon they were to close for a second time before yet another rescue attempt was successful.

When the second-round draw was made, all thoughts were for the Cinderella-club, Doncaster. Their reward was a home tie against Leeds and there was talk of a record turn-out at Tatters Field. Alas, it was not to be, and again the weather was to blame. Doncaster held out against financial incentives from their illustrious neighbours to switch the game to Headingley, the only safe place to play in such Arctic conditions. Offers of cash, coach ferries to run the Dons' fans into Leeds, bigger incentives – all were refused until, at last, Doncaster gave up home advantage. But they did not give up the fight. They pushed Leeds all the way before going down 10–28 and another piece of romance disappeared from the Challenge Cup story.

Elsewhere, likely candidates for Wembley were beginning to emerge. Castleford, with sixty points in the first round, faced what appeared to be a tricky trip to Barrow. No problem – they won handsomely by 30–6. Wigan and St Helens, the giants from west of the Pennines, met in what many Lancastrians had hoped would be a match reserved for Wembley itself. Wigan, inspired by the skills of the Australian Steve Ella, won 24–14.

Widnes, always candidates for a final place, shook off the challenge of emerging Rochdale Hornets while Oldham kept their heads against Warrington to win 13–6. Second-division Bramley almost took over from where Doncaster left off. They held troubled Bradford Northern 20–20, earned a replay at their own McLaren Field, but blew their second chance when they were crushed 2–36. And then there were eight . . .

'There are no easy games at this stage,' is the often-quoted standard reply from coaches when the quarter-final draw is made. Leigh were the sole survivors from the second division; Oldham were the only team of the eight who had never been to Wembley – and had not reached the semi-final for twenty-two years; Wigan, the game's biggest crowd-pullers, were still there; so, too,

12 David Liddiard, regarded as a winger in his native Australia, played mainly at full-back for Oldham where he had a superb season. Moreover, Liddiard's younger brother, Glen, was introduced to the first division at the age of sixteen and played exceptionally well for one so young. Here David Liddiard races away from his opposite full-back, Keith Mumby, in Oldham's 6–1 quarter-final Challenge Cup victory over Bradford Northern.

were the reigning league champions, Hull Kingston Rovers, highly fancied for the Cup as well. Widnes and Leeds, two of the game's great Cup fighters, were drawn to do battle together. And Bradford Northern were quietly moving along, ready for any slip-ups by the other clubs who were attracting most of the media attention. The critics were spoiled for choice. Should it be Widnes against Leeds? Or the holders Wigan against Castleford? Or even Oldham against Bradford Northern?

The Widnes *v.* Leeds game pulled in the thickest pad of scribes and they were not disappointed. A 10–10 draw meant that the teams had to go through it all again in a Headingley replay. Such a feast of Rugby League bordered on gluttony. Now news from other grounds filtered through and there was a shock. Holders Wigan were out, left at the side of the Wembley road by Castleford in front of 18,503 adoring Central Park fans. John Joyner, a servant of Castleford for fourteen years, and David Roockley, a team member for a lot less than that, were the try scorers as Wigan suffered their first home defeat since early season – and that was against Castleford too.

Oldham and Bradford Northern both found the going tough and the 6–1 score in Oldham's favour was a reflection of just how tight it all was. Over on Humberside, poor Leigh, disturbed by a dispute involving their Great Britain winger, Des Drummond, said goodbye to Wembley by slumping 10–25 to Hull KR. But the third round had not finished handing out its supply of drama. A mid-week visit to Headingley along with 15,000 other thrill-seekers was well worth the trip. There was not a try to be seen but even one would have been a slight and an injustice to the qualities of the defenders of both Leeds and Widnes. But 'no try' did not mean 'no thrills'. Two penalties and a drop goal took Leeds into the semi-finals. Somebody had to lose and, on the night, the 5–0 margin was just about right.

And so the 1986 Silk Cut Challenge Cup, after a shaky start weather-wise, a few boardroom rumblings during subsequent rounds (again with the weather the main enemy) and the sort of occasional surprises perpetrated by Doncaster, Bramley and the quietly all-conquering Castleford, moved on to the semi-finals.

One step from Wembley and the biggest day of a Rugby League player's life. Players would be flown 12,000 miles from Australia for that one game. That one game would be beamed live to the television screens of Australia. That one game ... the be-all and end-all of world Rugby League.

But before that the semi-finals. We had already seen enough thrills and all-action rugby to satisfy even the most hard-to-please critic. Surely the semi-finals would be a bit of an anti-climax? Not a bit of it, the Challenge Cup had still not overflowed. There was a lot more to come: Oldham would be paired with Castleford and Hull KR with Leeds.

The Challenge Cup Semi-final
Central Park, Wigan, 22 March
Castleford 18 Oldham 7

Would 1986 be Oldham's year? The only quarter-finalist never to have played at Wembley had reached the last four. One more bridge to cross. But did they have that extra that separates the forgotten men of losing semi-finalists from the finalists themselves?

There was no lack of optimism in the town. Oldham had not been in a Challenge Cup semi-final for twenty-two years and memories of that occasion, when they lost to Hull Kingston Rovers at the third attempt – one draw and one match abandoned because of failing light before eventual defeat – were brought flooding back. There was every reason to believe that they could go one better this time.

The people of Oldham were not trying to be disrespectful when they said, almost to a man, that had they been given the choice they would have settled for Castleford as semi-final opponents. After all, Castleford were saying the same about them! So everybody was happy enough when the teams trotted out at Wigan for the first semi-final. Oldham's Great Britain tourist, Terry Flanagan, made a plea for 15,000 fans to follow the team. Well, he did not quite get that but those who did travel to join the crowd of 12,430 certainly made themselves heard.

A Ray Ashton drop goal put the first point on Wigan's electric scoreboard as the two teams jostled for position, a little more serious than sparring partners but not yet ready for a fifteen-round bout. The Castleford scrum-half, Bob Beardmore, seized on the first major crack in the Oldham defence to cross for Castleford's first try and when Martin Ketteridge then added the goal to make the score 6–1 Oldham's dreams were looking exactly that . . . just dreams. But even the most ordinary of semi-finals will produce the occasional moment to remember and savour. At Wigan, it came via a sixteen-year-old Sydney schoolboy who had come to Britain on holiday, extended his stay, and won a place in a Challenge Cup semi-final team alongside his older brother.

Young Glen Liddiard teamed up with big brother David, the Oldham full-back, to conjure a try from nowhere on the stroke of half-time. It was Liddiard the elder who put in the telling kick across the Castleford line and the powerful legs of the younger which won the race for the touchdown. David Hobbs kicked the goal and Oldham led 7–6 at half-time. Those dreams were coming to life again.

But how twisted can fate become? Heroes can turn into villains in less time than it takes to recover from the backslapping. So it was with David Liddiard. For so long, he and brother Glen had been the double-pronged attack Oldham had used to counter the challenge of classy Castleford. But then young Glen became a concussion victim and played no further part in the game after half-time. For David it was the beginning of a nightmare. 'If it had not happened, David Liddiard would have won the player-of-the-match award easily,' said the Oldham coach, Frank Myler, of the incident that was to turn a Cup semi-final on its head and take Castleford to Wembley.

It was a kick from Bob Beardmore that started the problem. High, long ... and not too dangerous. Liddiard was under it comfortably. He waited ... and waited. Then, unaccountably, he allowed the ball to bounce and in one of those strange tricks of fate – an oval ball should bounce one way but doesn't – it did not cross the dead-ball line. Instead, it spun over Liddiard's head just as Beardmore arrived. It was Beardmore who reached the ball first, touched down ... and Castleford were on their way to Wembley. Referee Ronnie Campbell explained afterwards: 'The only person who could have scored that try was Beardmore, the kicker. If anybody else had touched down they would have been off-side.' Liddiard the elder shouldered the responsibility for the error. Manfully, he did not try to hide.

It was Bob Beardmore who was now the hero of Central Park. The try had changed the whole tone of the game. Oldham were never quite the same after that. Tony Marchant, Castleford's Great Britain centre, who only a few weeks earlier had scored on his international début against France on the same ground, added another try to his collection. But it did not seem to matter. The damage to Oldham had already been done. The sting had gone out of them. Scrum-half Ray Ashton ruined his own day by getting himself sent-off after the final whistle for an incident with the referee in the tunnel. And a small section of the crowd tried to spoil the occasion by fighting on the pitch long after the teams had reached their dressing-rooms.

While the incident left a sour taste, it was nothing to the taste that lingered with the Liddiard brothers. Defeat in a semi-final – especially after twenty-two years – is the worst taste of all. Along the corridor, the champagne was sweet. Castleford, unsung despite their excellent win over Wigan and the ninety points they had piled up against Hunslet and Barrow in earlier rounds, were going back to Wembley after a lapse of sixteen years. Tiny Jamie Sandy and the strong-running forward, Ian French, would be flying home before the final. But they would be back.

It was a victory that meant even more to the town than it did to the club, observed Castleford's chairman, David Poulter. The community, still recovering from the miners' strike, needed something to lift their spirits, and a visit to Wembley was just the job.

Castleford: Roockley; Plange, Marchant, Payne, Sandy; Joyner, Bob Beardmore; Ward, Horton, Johnson, Ketteridge, England, French

Substitutes: Mountain for England after 71 minutes, Hyde not used

Scorers: tries – Bob Beardmore (2), Marchant; goals – Ketteridge (3)

Oldham: David Liddiard; M'Barki, Foy, Warnecke, Taylor; Glen Liddiard, Ashton; Jones, Sanderson, Hobbs, Worrall, Graham, Flanagan

Substitutes: Parrish for Glen Liddiard and Nadiole for Flanagan at half-time, Flanagan for Sanderson after 66 minutes

Scorers: try – Glen Liddiard; goal – Hobbs; drop goal – Ashton

Referee. R. Campbell (Widnes)

Attendance: 12,430

The Challenge Cup Semi-final
Elland Road, Leeds, 29 March
Hull KR 24 Leeds 24

There comes a time in every sports lover's life when he sees a game, a race, a contest, a bout, that will serve him all his days. Such an occasion arrived at Elland Road, Leeds, on Easter Saturday, 1986 – the day of the Boat Race. It was a Rugby League Challenge Cup semi-final to beat them all.

Nobody thought it possible, but here we had a match that was even better than the previous year's Cup final at Wembley, suggested John Robinson of the *Sunday People*. He could not find a single person in the 23,866 crowd who would have dreamed of arguing with that. The contestants were the reigning league champions, Hull Kingston Rovers, and born-again Leeds under the awesome and inspiring influence of Peter Fox.

Mr Fox is not everyone's favourite coach and when he arrived at Leeds after a lengthy spell of success at nearby Bradford there were those among the critics who did more than just whisper a suggestion that the meat of Odsal could well be the poison of Headingley. But whatever his failings in the public relations department, Peter Fox is a winner inside the dressing-room and out on the training-ground where it matters most of all.

Leeds were again bubbling with enthusiasm, going for Wembley, pushing – albeit as outsiders – for the Slalom Lager Championship, and just as important, drawing sizeable crowds back to their Headingley terracing. Hull KR's quality has not been questioned for years. They had held the league title for two seasons under their popular coach, Roger Millward, they had in their ranks men of stature, Fairbairn, Dorahy, Smith, and Miller to name but a few. For Leeds there was Heron, playing once again like an international, the ageless Ward as hooker, young Powell in the front row. And, of course, Jeff Grayshon who had followed his old boss from Bradford to Leeds.

Grayshon, aged thirty-seven, was recalled in the same season to inspire Great Britain to a heart-warming Test series draw against the cream of New Zealand. He had never played at Wembley. Would the gods be kind to him at last? If they were, they would have to be cruel to George Fairbairn, the Scot who had played for two of the game's most illustrious clubs – Hull KR and Wigan – but had been at the wrong one when each of those clubs had reached the great and final stage.

A penalty each – one for Creasser, one for Dorahy – provided tasty starters before the main course. Hague and Heron linked up, Rovers were stretched and Creasser was on a run for the corner. Fairbairn chased and flung himself across in desperation. Creasser touched down ... Leeds 6, Hull KR 2. Webb, one of six Australians on semi-final duty, dropped a goal ... Leeds 7, Hull KR 2.

Currie, another Australian, cut through the Rovers' defence and headed for the line. Harkin, the tiny, tigerish scrum-half, lunged across with a mixture of desperation and frustration. But Currie kept his feet and his head, staggered forward and touched down ... Leeds 11, Hull KR 2. Referee Robin Whitfield signalled the try and then pointed towards the dressing-rooms. Harkin, for what he later admitted was 'a bad foul', had been sensationally sent off.

Creasser's goal attempt hit the post although in a matter of minutes a drop goal from Lyons was up there in electric lights ... Leeds 12, Hull KR 2. Surely Rovers, down to twelve men and down by ten points, were on their way out. They had lost forward Chris Burton with a broken arm, they had lost Harkin and, in truth, they were losing their discipline. Some of the tackles were, to say the least, a bit high although both sides contributed to this single flaw in a memorable match. Referee Whitfield could never be accused of being over-strict. Nevertheless, the game continued to flow without ever appearing to be in danger of exploding.

Hull KR gradually re-discovered their greatest asset, their total professionalism, and just before half-time winger David Laws pounced on one of the rare openings to appear in front of the Leeds line. Later film evidence suggested that Laws may not have grounded the ball correctly as he dived over in the corner but a try was given, referee Whitfield not having the luxury of slow-motion video re-runs and stills to assist him ... Leeds 12, Hull KR 6.

Half-time, just ten minutes for a breather – and that was just for the spectators! Out on the field the players returned to a royal welcome. They had earned it.

The second half.

Rovers brought on Gordon Smith (a scrum-half) to replace Andy Kelly (a forward). A wise move considering that Harkin was a scrum-half and had not been adequately replaced from the twelve players left on the field.

It was handy for the pressmen that they kept back some superlatives to describe the next forty minutes. They would need them. For eight minutes it was merely another epic cup-tie. After that it defied adequate description. Laws, scorer of the first Rovers try, repeated his contribution in the forty-eighth minute and by the time the game was an hour old the score, amazingly, was Leeds 14 Hull KR 24!

Mike Smith, an excellent centre who had given ten years' stalwart service to the Craven Park club, never contributed more than he did in those few breathtaking minutes at the start of the second half. Twice he cut through the Leeds defence on supercharged runs that brought tries and turned certain defeat into near-certain victory. But Leeds under Peter Fox are not the Leeds of a few years ago, all top show and soft centre. This lot did not know they were supposed to be losing a Cup semi-final! Currie rounded off a long bout of Leeds pressure that included some classic back play for a try that reduced the gap to a manageable six points. Creasser kicked the goal ... Leeds 20, Hull KR 24.

But no fairy-tale is complete without its Prince Charming. Up strode a young man in the blue and gold of Leeds to fit the bill perfectly. Nineteen-year-old bank clerk Paul Medley may be destined to become one of the great players of the future. On Easter Saturday 1986 he became today's man. Bursting through the tiring tacklers who made up Rovers' last line of defence, the teenage second-row forward collapsed over the line, ball in arms, for the try that saved the match. Creasser missed the kick at goal. Others – David Ward and John Dorahy in particular – missed drop goal attempts.

And quite right, too. This unforgettable semi-final could have had only one result: Leeds 24, Hull Kingston Rovers 24.

And a replay to come ...

Hull KR: Fairbairn; Clark, Mike Smith, Prohm, Laws; Dorahy, Harkin; Johnston, Watkinson, Ema, Burton, Hogan, Miller

Substitutes: Kelly for Burton after 25 minutes, Gordon Smith for Kelly at half-time, Kelly for Hogan after 79 minutes

Scorers: tries – Laws (2), Mike Smith (2); goals – Dorahy (4)

Leeds: Wilkinson; Andy Smith, Creasser, Currie, Gibson; Hague, Lyons; Grayshon, Ward, Powell, Kevin Rayne, Webb, Heron

Substitutes: Keith Rayne for Webb and Medley for Kevin Rayne after 53 minutes

Scorers: tries – Creasser, Currie (2), Medley; goals – Creasser (3); drop goals – Webb, Lyons

Referee: R. Whitfield (Widnes)

Attendance: 23,866

The Challenge Cup Semi-final Replay
Elland Road, Leeds, 3 April
Hull KR 17 Leeds 0

For forty minutes things were just too good to be true. When Hull Kingston Rovers and Leeds met at Elland Road for the second time in five days, this time in front of a crowd of 32,485, the first half was every bit as exciting and thrill-packed as the previous Saturday's non-stop draw. Played at breakneck speed with hardly a stoppage for a scrum or foul or minor casualty, there was hardly time to draw breath from one crunching tackle or sparkling run to the next. One hundred and twenty minutes of Rugby League action ended with the two teams still locked together, not a point between them.

Paul Harkin, sent off on Saturday, became the Thursday-night star with a drop goal to open the scoring in the first minute of the second half. It was a pity it had to happen. Things were never quite the same again. It was still a good match, still full of exciting action and entertainment, but somehow not quite the same after that point.

So often it has been said about a game that 'it needs a try to liven it up'. At Elland Road, just the opposite happened – a try was an intrusion into deadly combat of two teams visibly weakening under the strain of offering memorable entertainment to customers who, over five days, had paid out £200,000 to be counted among the privileged. Why did somebody have to lose?

That somebody was Leeds. With Phil Hogan, Harkin and the ever-active Miller in full flight, a try came. It was from Peter Johnston, one of the lesser known of the Australian imports, and it was the score that finally nudged Leeds beyond recovery. Dorahy missed a simple kick but soon added a penalty to make the score 7–0.

Leeds were now desperate, and the growing feeling that it was not to be their night gained even more strength when they were awarded a penalty. Needing to score twice to survive, they settled for a kick at goal. Normally young David Creasser would have chalked up two points with a minimum of difficulty. This time he shot wide and Leeds were still seven points adrift. That margin was stretched even wider when John Lydiat caught the Leeds defence unawares. He nipped in for the touchdown and his jig of delight became, in effect, a dance of victory.

Andy Kelly later added another try and Dorahy another goal but they were incidentals to the main script. A 17–0 score looks like the result of a one-sided no-contest. Nobody at Elland Road that Thursday night will believe that for a moment.

And so to Wembley.

Hull KR: Fairbairn; Clark, Mike Smith, Prohm, Laws; Dorahy, Harkin; Johnston, Watkinson, Ema, Kelly, Hogan, Miller

Substitutes: Lydiat for Prohm after 33 minutes, Gordon Smith for Harkin after 68 minutes

Scorers: tries – Johnston, Lydiat, Kelly; goals – Dorahy (2); drop goal – Harkin

Leeds: Wilkinson; Andy Smith, Creasser, Currie, Gibson; Hague, Lyons; Grayshon, Ward, Powell, Medley, Kevin Rayne, Heron

Substitutes: Keith Rayne for Kevin Rayne and Webb for Medley after 58 minutes

Referee: R. Whitfield (Widnes)

Attendance: 32,485

The Challenge Cup Final
Wembley Stadium, 3 May
Castleford 15 Hull KR 14

It was a final that many of the game's pundits reckoned would be a private affair for Yorkshire eyes only. Castleford, the homespun (save for a couple of Aussies) underdogs, against Hull Kingston Rovers, the team that those same pundits would have backed for a trip to Wembley as long ago as the first day of the season.

Predictable and fashionable against the unpredictable and unfashionable. The haves versus the have-nots. But, for all that attraction of opposites, a private affair not worth a mention west of the Pennines. How wrong can you be? An 82,000 crowd paid world-record Rugby League receipts of £806,000 for the privilege of gate-crashing that private affair.

On the roads to Wembley on 3 May were the coats of many colours. The gold and black of Castleford and the red and white of Hull KR stood out ... but in there somewhere were the black and white of the arch-enemies Hull; the blue of champions Halifax; the cherry and white of fallen favourites Wigan; the all-black of recently rescued Fulham and dozens more who had made the long trek south for Rugby League's gala day. It was a royal Wembley too. Princess Alexandra would be there to present the famous old trophy to the winning captain. No interest outside Yorkshire? Somebody had to be joking! Rugby League fans in Sydney would be staying up half the night to watch a live transmission of a match that, whatever else they can show us in the Sydney league, is an act they cannot follow.

Wembley was, as it always is on Cup final day, a sea of colour, of smiling friendly faces, of families on day trips enjoying the occasion. On the pitch there was the now familiar schoolboy match as curtain raiser. Behind the scenes, though, the Hull KR camp was certainly not full of smiling faces. Peter Johnston, their young Australian, had spent a sleepless night; Gavin Miller, their potential match-winner, had suffered a hamstring injury in the final training session. Less than an hour before the kick-off the Wembley press-box was still full of uncertain reporters waiting to hear the Hull KR team. Castleford, meanwhile, had managed to sleep the sleep of the underdog. No problems there.

Two of the best friends in the game – Castleford's Malcolm Reilly and Hull KR's Roger Millward – headed the columns of players up the tunnel and on to the field to the familiar roar of the crowd. It was too much to expect a repeat of the previous season's Challenge Cup final when Wigan beat Hull 28–24. But Wembley has a habit of coming up with a special occasion ... and the drama of the closing stages of the 1986 final will long be remembered by the vast crowd and millions of TV viewers.

But, first things first. Rovers, who had looked far from happy on the Friday afternoon Wembley walkabout that teams undertake each year to get the feel of the place, still looked out of sorts. The tag of strong favourites appeared to hang heavily round their necks. Miller, strangely subdued (it was only revealed later that the gamble on his hamstring trouble had been taken) and strangely quiet. At half-back the ebullient Harkin and 'Joe Cool' Dorahy were ineffective. Even-so, it took Castleford twenty minutes to cash in. And then it came in the spectacular style for which Wembley occasions have become

13 Tony Marchant, Castleford's Great Britain centre, opens the scoring in the Challenge Cup final after a magnificent sprint to the line. Hull KR's David Laws arrives on the scene too late.

famous. The powerful prop, Kevin Ward, made the initial surge through the first line of Rovers' cover. He is nicknamed 'The Beast' – but his pass was a beauty! It sent in the international centre, Tony Marchant, and, for once, the dependable George Fairbairn failed to obey the golden rule ... he bought the dummy. The line in front of Marchant was open and in he went for the first try of the game. Martin Ketteridge kicked the goal and Castleford were six points in front.

Dorahy restored Hull KR's self-belief with a forty-yard penalty after England had fouled Mike Smith. The gap was down to a manageable four points before scrum-half Bob Beardmore landed a drop goal. Rovers were then in desperate need of inspiration ... or luck, and they got a huge slice of the latter just before half-time. The second-row forward, Andy Kelly, had not recovered his ground when, suddenly, he found the ball in his hands ... courtesy of a pass from Castleford's England. Kelly had the eager Prohm in

14 Ian French, the tall, superbly athletic Australian loose forward, had an outstanding season for Castleford and his performance in the Challenge Cup final against a subdued Hull KR side was as good as any he had given.

15 Jamie Sandy, the versatile Australian stand-off or wing, was flown back from Brisbane especially to play on the left wing for Castleford in the Challenge Cup final. He delighted his enthusiastic supporters as well as himself by scoring Castleford's third and winning try. Here Sandy takes a pass from his stand-off, John Joyner, and begins his great try-scoring run.

support and there was little to do but feed the New Zealander and watch him race for the line. Dorahy missed the goal-kick but Rovers went in only a point down. It was a situation they could hardly claim to have earned. But if they thought the worst was over ... well, it just wasn't their day.

Beardmore, who was clearly having the better of the tussle of two highly ranked scrum-halves, struck again two minutes after the interval. His short kick ahead, which he later described as merely a ploy to put pressure on Rovers and in no way designed to bring a try, produced another blow for Rovers. As Beardmore followed up, the covering Prohm appeared to be far too casual and Beardmore pounced to seize his chance. The touchdown made the score 11–6 and Hull KR saw the Challenge Cup slipping away for the second time.

Worse was to come. With the game an hour old, Jamie Sandy – nicknamed Tom Thumb – stretched out his 5 feet 4 inch frame on a diagonal run that caught Hull KR flapping. The little Australian almost disappeared under a pile of bodies as he reached the line. But he came up all smiles. He had flown 12,000 miles for that ... a try at Wembley. There was a minor skirmish (so out of character on a truly sporting occasion) but when the dust settled the excellent Robin Whitfield was still in charge. Could Rovers achieve in the final eighteen minutes what they had failed to do in the previous hour – find the form that had made them the most feared team on any fixture list?

They improved and in the sixty-eighth minute Prohm was on hand to make up for his earlier tardiness by scoring the Humbersiders' second try. The goalkick was too difficult for Dorahy, but, only five points down, Rovers now had the chance that seemed to have long gone. Castleford needed all their grit to stem the red tide that suddenly threatened them. Dorahy foolishly threw a punch at a Castleford player when it would have been far wiser to ignore the opponent and the relieving penalty saved Castleford on that occasion.

As the minutes ticked away, you could sense there was more to come, that this 1986 Cup final had not breathed its last. And so it came, in the minutes that were being added on for an unfortunate earlier injury to young Harrison, the Hull KR forward. In injury time, with the Castleford fans whistling and cheering for the final hooter, the substitute Lydiat found an opening, right in the corner, near the flag, and in he went. Castleford 15, Hull KR 14.

It was all up to Dorahy. Carefully he built his mound of sand. Even more carefully, he tested three footballs before making his choice. It was a difficult kick at the best of times. No space for a run up, next to the touchline. And at Wembley, that simply made it ten times worse.

The Castleford team dared not look. They could only listen for the crowd reaction. When it came – a sure sign that Dorahy's kick was wide – the relief of the gold-shirted players was almost tangible. Rovers hurried back to their positions and Castleford did not delay. There was a flurry of activity but it was merely the epilogue. The last act had been completed and, in fairness, justice had been served by Dorahy's miss. He could not be blamed. Indeed, the kick was as difficult as any there have been.

John Joyner was the captain who collected the Cup from Princess Alexandra and he said afterwards: 'It's a pity not every professional player can have this feeling at least once in his career.' Bob Beardmore collected the Lance Todd Trophy as man-of-the-match ahead of his team-mate Kevin Ward. But one of the lasting memories of a dramatic Cup final was the sight of beaten coach Roger Millward in the winners' dressing-room. Amid the noise of singing and champagne corks popping, his friend Malcolm Reilly called for silence. Millward, visibly shaken by the defeat, said simply: 'Thanks for the game, lads. The better team won the day.'

It was a fitting end to another great Rugby League day.

Castleford: Lord; Plange, Marchant, Hyde, Sandy; Joyner, Bob Beardmore; Ward, Kevin Beardmore, Johnson, England, Ketteridge, French

Substitutes: Roockley for Lord after 63 minutes, Horton for Kevin Beardmore after 74 minutes

Scorers: tries – Marchant, Bob Beardmore, Sandy; goal – Ketteridge; drop goal – Bob Beardmore

Hull KR: Fairbairn; Clark, Mike Smith, Prohm, Laws; Dorahy, Harkin; Johnston, Watkinson, Ema, Kelly, Harrison, Miller

Substitutes: Lydiat for Harrison after 56 minutes: Gordon Smith for Kelly after 68 minutes

Scorers: tries – Prohm (2), Lydiat; goal – Dorahy

Referee: R. Whitfield (Widnes)

Attendance: 82,134

Peter Wilson

4

THE SLALOM LAGER CHAMPIONSHIP AND PREMIERSHIP TROPHY

THE SLALOM LAGER CHAMPIONSHIP

A major surprise of the season, albeit a most refreshing one, was to find Halifax on the top of the Slalom Lager championship table when the competition ended. It was a magnificent effort, and totally unexpected, for at the beginning of the season the Thrum Hall side were rank outsiders for the title. And odds of 150–1 did not seem particularly generous when they lost three and drew one of their first four matches. However, that turned out to be their worst run of the season. Halifax never again lost successive matches, and those who at the end of the season accused them of being 'lucky' should be reminded of the team's consistency right through the winter. Of course they had some luck but they 'bought' it with shrewd organization and planning and a lot of quality play.

As the season developed Halifax became a highly efficient team, success bringing tremendous self-belief and no little skill. Their Australians settled quickly and blended well with a series of new home signings. Chris Anderson was a top-class player-coach and received enthusiastic support, not only from the players, but also from the board.

They were probably fortunate to be beaten in the first rounds of the John Player Trophy and Silk Cut Challenge Cup. Consequently they were one of the few clubs to avoid the end-of-season pile-up of fixtures, caused by the horrendous winter, which certainly wrecked the hopes of Hull Kingston Rovers, who reached the finals of their three knock-out competitions. Yet even when Halifax went to the top of the table, there was always the feeling that

16 Halifax won the championship because, after an uncertain start, they developed into a highly efficient team, bolstered by tremendous self-belief and no little skill. They were led with imagination, shrewdness and a lot of quality play by their player-coach, Chris Anderson.

they might be overhauled, and it says much for their resilience that they hung on so well when pressure mounted.

Halifax were also prepared to take risks and this was where initiative came in. They played a home game against St Helens on 5 January at Headingley, won it and went to the top of the table for the first time. They played another home fixture, against Widnes, at the Halifax Town soccer ground. There they were beaten but it was another fixture less to play later and the team eventually felt the benefit. Perhaps their best performance came in a match they didn't win, at Wigan, when they drew 6–6 after scoring the only try. That game above all convinced Halifax and a great many others that they had the quality to go all the way and win the championship.

The club's energetic president, David Brook, had been criticized the previous season for his heavy recruitment in Australia but there is no doubt that his signings had helped to keep the side in the first division. With a limit of five non-British players in the 1985–86 season he had to be more selective and chose well. There was one set-back when the League ruled that Chris Anderson was an overseas player, for it meant that their forward, Keith Neller, a big success the previous season, was unable to play. But the men who did play were ideal. Full-back Joe Kilroy was an outstanding attacking player with his amazing knack of being able to ease his way through tackles. The props, Cavill Heugh and Geoff Robinson, set an awesome example in the front row with strong, direct running, and Heugh in particular had an exceptional ability to slip the ball away to his support players. Centre Tony Anderson had good pace and had clearly developed his attacking play from the previous season.

Some of the British players recruited by Halifax caused a few raised eyebrows but what great service they gave. The much-travelled scrum-half Gary Stephens had his best season for some years. He dovetailed perfectly with Chris Anderson, called the shots well and varied his tactics with skill. The second-row forward, Neil James, improved so rapidly that no one questioned his selection for Great Britain and he underlined it with the man-of-the-match award against France. Mick Scott, the lone survivor from the dark days when the club was beaten by the amateur side, Cawoods, thoroughly enjoyed himself; the loose forward, Paul Dixon, settled easily into the top bracket; and Welshman Brian Juliff played with typical enthusiasm on the wing and in the second row. During the season Colin Whitfield was signed from Wigan to bolster the squad and he scored some important points in the run-in to the championship, while the young hooker, Seamus McCallion, thrived on the pressure. Overall, the Halifax success was a welcome boost to what has always been referred to as a rugby town but with little chance to prove it in recent years. Attendances rocketed and they had a big away following all season.

The battle for top place involved a number of clubs for most of the season.

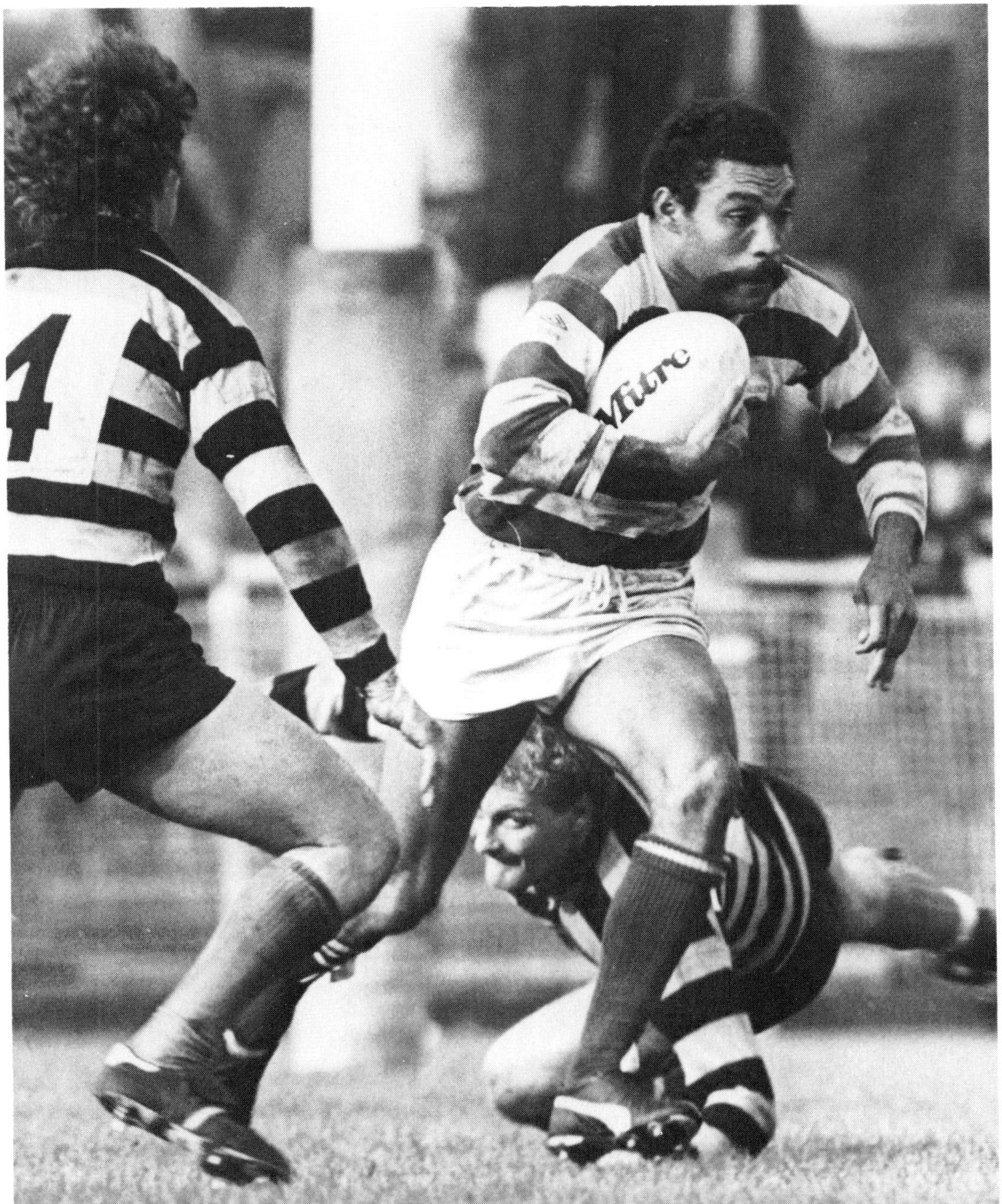

17 During the close season, Halifax again entered the Australian market and bought with commendable skill. Their full-back, Joe Kilroy, was an outstanding attacking player with an amazing knack of easing his way out of tackles.

18 The Australian prop forward Cavill Heugh was another inspired Halifax signing before the start of the season. With Geoff Robinson, yet another Australian, and the young hooker, Seamus McCallion, Heugh completed an awesome front row. He set a splendid example with his strong, direct running and by his ability to slip the ball away when under pressure to his support players.

Oldham were the leaders on Boxing Day, Widnes led for a time in February, and Wigan, Warrington, Leeds and Hull KR all had firm hopes of the title at some stage, while there was a tremendous late rush from St Helens. In the end it meant that Halifax needed a point from their last game, at home to Featherstone Rovers, who were still in relegation trouble. Wigan could still snatch the title if Halifax lost. The game against Rovers proved a fascinating affair, with Halifax apparently home and dry, leading 11–1, only for Rovers to stage a storming rally and level matters at 13–13. Suddenly the hooter went and Thrum Hall went mad. There were suggestions that the hooter had gone some three minutes early. There was certainly support for that view in Wigan but Halifax were champions and the point was enough to make Featherstone safe. Little wonder there were smiles all round.

Wigan were justified in feeling frustrated at finishing so close to the top. They seemed to have the championship well in hand after hitting form following a strange opening when they lost four of their first five matches. That state of affairs was never going to last. When the Australians Steve Ella and Greg Dowling moved smoothly in, along with Ellery Hanley, success was inevitable. Ella was electrifying, a devastating finisher with lightning pace off the mark. Dowling was a magnificent down-to-earth prop, again with superb ability to unload the ball. Andy Goodway had already been signed to strengthen the pack and it was like the old days when Wigan snapped up Joe Lydon from Widnes for £100,000 as well as the Springbok Rugby Union internationals Ray Mordt and Rob Louw. The fans loved it. They flocked to Central Park and formed a huge away following to benefit other clubs.

When winger Henderson Gill recovered from a broken ankle to add his special talents to the team, it seemed that Wigan could not be stopped. But they lurched badly around Easter when the title was there for the taking. They were beaten in the last minute by St Helens on Good Friday, suffered a crushing home defeat by Oldham on Easter Monday and three days later were held to a draw by Warrington at Central Park; suddenly the games they had in hand on Halifax had disappeared. Ella's departure for home brought the switch of Hanley to stand-off and he began to shoot up the try-scoring charts with his uncanny ability to support the break as well as making plenty of breaks of his own. Home products also were not ignored and the young centre, Richard Russell, looked a very promising player as did a sturdy prop forward, Ian Lucas. But Wigan's inconsistency at the end of the season let them down and they will always regard the 1985–86 trophy as the one that got away.

St Helens never really figured as a candidate for the title until a blistering late rush of thirteen successive victories shot them to third in the table. They caused a sensation in mid-season by appointing Alex Murphy as coach in place of Billy Benyon, who in the eyes of many supporters had done a sound job.

Murphy wasn't happy with the strength of the squad and soon made his feelings known. For a time the side struggled, and injury problems to the loose forward Harry Pinner did not help matters. The signing of the Kiwi centre, Mark Elia, brought to the side a finishing ability that had been lacking, despite the efforts of centre Brett French and the second-row forward Roy Haggerty. Chris Arkwright was another consistent and competitive performer, both at stand-off and loose forward, where he took over with some distinction from Pinner. Neil Holding had some bright moments and the Saints could also take some satisfaction from the work of younger players, such as Paul Round, Andy Platt and Paul Loughlin.

Warrington looked a fearsome outfit when they gathered together Les Boyd, Kevin Tamati and Alan Rathbone to add to the energetic efforts of Andy Gregory. Unfortunately, those three forwards did not play together as often as had been hoped and league progress was steady rather than exceptional. They came up with another exciting Australian in Phil Blake, an accomplished finisher, and perhaps with the 'find' of the season in half-back Paul Bishop. Bishop developed into a fine player. He was nippy in support, a good creative player and a sound goal-kicker. His future will be watched with interest. Among the disappointments for Warrington were the continued injury problems of their talented centre, Ronnie Duane, who did not come into the side regularly until late in the season and then showed how much his talents had been missed. Had Duane played through the season, Warrington would have gone much closer to league honours; and they also had to contend with the loss for more than half the season of their strong-running second-row forward, Bob Eccles. In the circumstances fourth place was creditable.

Widnes did well to stay in the hunt for so long in a season that was really a period of rebuilding for them. They were rarely able to play a settled team because of injury and suffered a shattering blow when their Australian centre, Steve Rogers, who could have brought Naughton Park to life, broke a leg after only thirteen minutes of his first match and did not play again. That was a dreadful set-back for Widnes and a big disappointment to the RL public generally. Kurt Sorensen had some typically robust matches as did the Australian, Noel Cleal, at times a fearsome runner who took a good deal of holding near the line. David Hulme played well at half-back and brother Paul looked a splendid prospect, while the loose forward, Richard Eyres, continued his development. Darren Wright has fine potential at centre, and generally the future looks good for Widnes, particularly if Tony Myler can prove that he is consistently the best stand-off in the country. The sale of Lydon to Wigan was a disappointment, explained by the board as a necessary measure because of financial problems. This did not appease the coach, Eric Hughes, who resigned and Doug Laughton returned to the post.

Leeds started the season with a new coach in Peter Fox, who was quick to point out that the reduction in the number of overseas players at the club meant that he had five fewer players in his squad. A severe blow was the retirement of the stand-off, John Holmes, who for nearly 600 matches had been quite outstanding in the Headingley colours. Leeds suffered a bad autumn spell but hit form in the new year, when the Australians, Tony Currie at centre and Cliff Lyons at scrum-half, showed their best form. Fox was never happy with the strength of the pack and turned to one of his old lieutenants from Bradford, the veteran prop Jeff Grayshon, for stability. Grayshon did just that, gave great service and belied his age by playing seven games in eighteen days in April. Leeds also paid a club record fee of £50,000 for the Batley three-quarter, Carl Gibson, who showed such flair that he is certain to excite Headingley supporters in years to come. However, other bids to strengthen the squad were unsuccessful. Two young players impressed: Roy Powell at prop and the teenager Paul Medley, who proved himself a devastating runner with a big future. Their new year revival left Leeds handily placed for the title until their mighty Challenge Cup battles against Widnes and Hull KR, both of which went to replays. After their semi-final defeat by Rovers the league season turned sour and despite having played home fixtures on the heated Headingley pitch during the worst part of the winter, they still faced a fixture pile-up.

It is becoming clear that the first division is either too big or the end-of-season deadline too early. This was the problem for Hull KR, who finished seventh due to an appalling backlog of matches following their successful progress in the Challenge Cup and John Player Trophy. Rovers reached the finals of three major competitions, which meant that much of their league programme had to be crammed into the last month of the season. To have to play five home games in nine days, a third of their home league season, was patently unfair on season ticket holders. To add to their problems, they had to endure torrential rain during those last days and, with postponement out of the question, had to play when their Craven Park pitch was clearly unfit.

Rovers were superbly led by their loose forward, Gavin Miller, and he had marvellous support from the scrum-half, Paul Harkin. George Fairbairn was always a sturdy contributor and there were some glorious touches from John Dorahy. Mike Smith retained his knack of popping up in the right place to snatch important tries, there was tidy work from David Laws on the wing and John Lydiat was an excellent squad man. Des Harrison showed promise among the younger players and for sheer consistency of effort no one did better than Zook Ema in a largely unsung role. The leadership of captain and hooker David Watkinson was also important and the general view was that Rovers were the most professional side in the league.

Hull's season never really took off. They were hit by long absences through injury to Garry Schofield, and once again their prop, Trevor Skerrett, had injury problems. Calls to Test duty for their Kiwi contingent meant a series of fixture postponements and these contributed to upsetting the team's rhythm. Their scrum-half, Andy Gascoigne, with the onerous task of replacing the brilliant Australian, Peter Sterling, looked a bargain signing from Bramley; but he too was hit by injury. Amid all this Lee Crooks had a splendid season up front, while Gary Kemble and James Leuluai were sound if not spectacular. Numerous young players were introduced and the full-back, Steve Hick, and the winger, Michael Brand, showed rich promise.

Hull's season moved in fits and starts but a crushing John Player Trophy defeat at St Helens, followed quickly by another upset at Swinton in the league, brought a storm of criticism in some quarters and their coach, Arthur Bunting, resigned, ending a distinguished period at the Boulevard. Ken Foulkes took over and worked hard to restore confidence but a first-round Cup-tie defeat away to Hull KR meant that their Wembley hopes finished early. It was a season of catching breath for Hull after a whirlwind few years and attendances dipped sharply, the situation not helped by the demands of the Ground Safety Act, which meant the closure for a time of the Boulevard's most famous monument, the Threepenny Stand.

Oldham's failure even to qualify for the Premiership after leading the table in mid-season was a bitter disappointment for their fans. So often they appear to be on the edge of success but fade in the last quarter of the season. Their initiative in snapping up the much sought-after Australian second-row forward, Mal Graham, was a big success. He showed rare finishing ability to collect twenty-one tries. David Liddiard, regarded as a winger in Australia, was superb at full-back, despite ill-luck with injury. A brilliant player, he added much needed attacking flair to the side and when he was missing some of the sparkle disappeared. Liddiard's brother, Glen, was introduced to the first division at the age of sixteen and was in no way over-awed either on the wing or at stand-off. Much more will be heard of this young man.

Salford were happy to finish tenth, for they had by no means a big pack, and their position might have been higher still had their talented stand-off Neil Baker, another Australian, stayed longer. Baker scored some delightful solo tries with his ability to chip the ball over the top and follow up at speed and he helped bring confidence to the backs. His scrum-half partner, Darren Bloor, emerged from the season with considerable credit and did well enough to catch the eye of the Great Britain coach, Maurice Bamford, and gain selection to his squad to meet the Kangaroos in the autumn of 1986. Their loose forward, John Pendlebury, worked well as did the energetic Mick McTigue, and Ged Byrne had some good moments at centre.

Castleford's season was like so many at Wheldon Road in recent years, a scramble to avoid relegation that made nonsense of the talent at the club. Panic was eased once again by a good Cup run and this time they overcame the semi-final hurdle. Their second-row forward Martin Ketteridge came on in leaps and bounds in his first full season and the busy hooker, Stuart Horton, was a highly competent stand-in for the international, Kevin Beardmore, during the latter's lengthy absence through injury. The consistency and spirit of their leading try-scorer, Tony Marchant, earned him a Great Britain place; a summer in Australia could prove of enormous benefit to this enthusiastic and capable three-quarter. Kevin Ward was at times a towering figure up front with willing support from the underrated Keith England.

Castleford also recruited in Australia, bringing over a loose forward, Ian French, and the utility back, Jamie Sandy. French, a superbly athletic player like so many Australian forwards, had his best moments in the Cup but he gave some good league displays as well with his direct running and strong cover tackling. Sandy played at full-back, stand-off and on the wing without quite making the same impact but had some good days, especially at No. 6. However, the success of French in the back three meant that the captain, John Joyner, was able to revert to stand-off, where he seemed more effective with his handling skills and sound defence. However, the puzzle remains why this team, so talented on their day, should always have to struggle in the league.

Perhaps a season of struggle for Bradford Northern was no real surprise. Things started badly with problems over their superstar, Ellery Hanley, and his departure to Wigan was a blow, even though Northern gained two sound three-quarters, Steve Donlan and Phil Ford, as well as cash. They signed John Woods for stand-off, although Odsal officials were at pains to stress that the aim had been to play Woods and Hanley together, not sell one to buy the other. Woods fared well as goal-kicker but his true attacking skills were seen only in flashes as the side struggled against relegation. The sale of big Jeff Grayshon to Leeds also cost the pack its leader, though Brian Noble had a spirited season. Northern caused a sensation when they signed the Welsh Rugby Union international scrum-half and captain, Terry Holmes, and it was a tragedy that the only immediate benefit was in publicity. Holmes made his début at Swinton, who were more than happy to stage the game, but was taken off with a damaged shoulder after only thirteen minutes. Holmes tried again in the second team but once more failed to last the eighty minutes as he suffered further shoulder problems. Northern were justifiably upset and felt they were being sneered at by some people for signing a player reputed to have had injury problems in his Union days. The truth is that many in Rugby League were sad to see such enterprise meeting so many early set-backs. There are few players of his charisma around and everyone in Rugby League would have benefited in some way had things worked out favourably. However, Holmes can and surely

19 One of the saddest sights of the season was the departure from the field with a damaged shoulder of Terry Holmes, the Welsh international RU captain, after only thirteen minutes of his first Rugby League match against Swinton. Holmes had been signed by Bradford Northern in a blaze of publicity and was not to play again in the first division during the season.

will add much to the Odsal scene for the departure of Hanley has left supporters desperate for a new hero.

Featherstone Rovers faced the very real danger of relegation for most of the season, ensuring safety only in that dramatic last match at Halifax. They were basically too good to go down but had some nightmare spells when their defence fell apart. They signed prop forward Karl Harrison from Bramley to strengthen the pack and paid a club record £50,000 to York for their stand-off, Graham Steadman, when safety was in doubt. The gamble paid off, Steadman linked well with Deryck Fox, and this half-back pairing could yet prove one of the best in the league if they get the chance to play without relegation pressures. Fox had a fine season in difficult circumstances; now the worry for Rovers must be what effect a hard season in Australia will have on his stamina. Steadman has the ability to conjure tries out of nothing and there was a good season from loose forward Paul Lyman, who worked hard and finished with eighteen tries, a praiseworthy tally in a struggling side. Fox, Steadman and Lyman could form a midfield triangle to match the best if Rovers are in the right mood.

The trio of clubs to be relegated brought no surprises for York, Swinton and Dewsbury were always going to struggle without an injection of expensive talent. None had the cash for such ventures and their teams were really too inexperienced to cope week in and week out with the pressures of the first division. However, they can take encouragement from the fact that they produced some good performances on occasion and several young players did well in the circumstances.

For quite a time York looked as if they might survive and even had a spell in mid-table. But this was when such capable Australians as their full-back, Rod Pethybridge, who was surprisingly released by Featherstone when they decided to concentrate purely on home-produced players, their prop, Mike Marketo, and the utility player, Matt Carter, were in their ranks. When the dreaded deadline arrived for contracted Australians to return home, York, who had taken a big gamble not to run an 'A' team, were left badly exposed with their senior squad simply not big enough. The sale of Steadman had also left a gap that couldn't really be plugged. They needed to win their last two games against the bottom club, Dewsbury, and at home to out-of-form Leeds to have a hope of surviving. They were forced to play half-fit men at Dewsbury and were beaten and, with the cause lost, four trialists turned out against Leeds. The first division is too demanding for that. Yet their scrum-half, Steve Dobson, had a splendid season, playing so much of it without experienced forward cover, and their second-row forward, Gary Price, also showed consistency of effort.

If Swinton had been told at the beginning of the season that they would beat Widnes, Hull and Hull KR, they would have fancied their chances of survival. But these were all-too-rare glimpses of sunlight in a dark season. The side was badly hit by lengthy injuries to such as Martin Lee, Danny Wilson, who scarcely played all season, and Jeff Brown, which meant too many others learning the hard way. They found an excellent young scrum-half in Tony Hewitt, and Paul Topping had a steady season at full-back. In the end the Station Road club had to look to their second team for consolation and winning the Slalom Lager Alliance Cup should offer hope for the future.

Dewsbury also lacked experience, despite the efforts of Nigel Stephenson, and they lost David Busfield early on when he gave up the fight against a series of knee injuries. They experienced some ill-luck in two or three home matches but in several away ones the defence was horribly exposed. Here, too, a promising young scrum-half, Mark Keyworth, emerged with a good deal of credit from a thankless task. The prop, Paul Broxholme, showed distinct potential and their reserve winger, John Moore, came into the senior side at full-back and produced some very good displays, notably the team's only hat-trick of tries in the season in the belated win over York.

The indications from the first division, however, were that even the reduction to three up and three down is still one too many. Promoted clubs are either going to have to recruit extensively on home soil or in Australia in the hope of snatching enough points for survival before the end of March. Unfortunately the British winter makes that a gamble.

No one needed a crystal ball or the brain of the season to pick out two of the promotion certainties in the second division. It would have been a sensation had Leigh and Barrow, both relegated the previous season, not bounced straight back. Leigh did so with a vengeance, despite the sudden departure of Alex Murphy to St Helens. He was replaced by Tommy Dickens, who had done such a sturdy job at Blackpool Borough and there was no loss of momentum. In fact the Hilton Park side's return to the top bracket was never more than a formality; they had far too much pace for the second division and some of their matches were almost an embarrassment. They topped fifty points in six of their league matches, reaching a peak with a massive ninety-two against a hapless Keighley team. It was little wonder that they went on to create a new second-divison record of 1,156 points during the season.

Leigh's only defeat came at Barrow, 2–14, in September, and from that point they registered thirty successive victories, another record. Leigh's three-quarters scored the points, particularly the centres. Steve Halliwell, English-born but recruited from Australia, was always prominent and finished with a positive blaze of tries, twenty-one in the last eight matches to top the league's list for the season with forty-nine. All except one came in league games to create a new record for the division. His tally included a five, inevitably in the game against Keighley, and three fours. John Henderson was never far behind. This fine prospect might also have topped the forty mark had he not ended the season early to spend the summer in Australian rugby. He finished with thirty-one tries and his progress in the first division will be carefully watched, for he is rated highly by many experts. The full-back, Chris Johnson, also enjoyed himself. He landed a club record of 173 goals, two of them drop goals, and scored exactly 400 points, yet another club best. The Test winger, Des Drummond, had a few problems, being dropped and later suspended at one stage during his testimonial season, but later made his peace. He collected twenty-one tries as well as learning that coach Dickens cannot make exceptions regarding non-attendance at training even for star players. Drummond's fellow winger, Phil Fox, scored twenty-nine tries and his tally, too, included a five, in the John Player Trophy tie at Batley. The Australian stand-off, Trevor Cogger, looked very good in the first part of the season and the young forward, Wayne Atherton, showed rich promise.

Barrow also topped 1,000 points during the second-division season, they and Leigh helping to make out a strong case for three divisions. Their season, too, would have been very impressive but for a stumble around Easter when they lost three games out of four. The Cumbrian club took the precaution also of recruiting in Australia and had particularly good service from the Test prop Dave Brown and his fellow front-row forward, Tony Elliott. In fact the outstanding play of Australian front-row players generally during the British season gave much food for thought. Steve Tickle had a sound and consistent season at full-back as did Stewart Williams, who topped the club list with twenty-seven tries. Norman Turley had some good matches and the scrum-half, David Cairns, was always busy and effective. The club signed Brian Blacker from Huddersfield late in the season to strengthen the backs and did not need telling that safety in the first division next season must to a large extent depend on another trip to the Australian market.

The tussle for third place was trimmed down to three clubs, Wakefield Trinity, Whitehaven and Rochdale Hornets, with Trinity overcoming a few alarming displays to finish comfortably clear of their rivals. The Trinity coach, Len Casey, went back to his old club for experience. David Hall played for him for a spell and Roy Holdstock for a longer period but his long-term signing was Tracey Lazenby, who gave good service in the back three and at stand-off on occasions. Their experience helped to bring the best out of the capable centre, Phil Eden, and there was willing work from the forwards, Ian Hopkinson and Gary Cocks. It was a pity that injury prevented more being seen of the lively half-back, Stuart Wainman, and fire-service duties took the talented full-back, Gary Spencer, out of the game for some months.

Whitehaven looked a sound bet for promotion for much of the season but ended with a horrifying run of only two wins from their last eight matches to suggest that they really need a further season in the lower sphere in which to rebuild. A start was made in April with the signing of the Welsh Rugby Union international centre, Bob Ackerman, a deal which raised quite a few eyebrows. He joined a back division containing such bright young players as Mark Beckwith and Jim Dalton, although the talented Vince Gribbin missed most of the season. There was a bright first half of the season from the young prop, Jeff Simpson, and the scrum-half, Graham Cameron, showed up well in the second half. But the Cumbrians will have to strengthen their forwards to make a really effective challenge in the future.

Rochdale Hornets started the season with a new board of directors, led by an energetic and outspoken young chairman in Fred Wood, and virtually recruited a new team with signings from home and abroad. There were three Australians, Tony and Greg Austin and Phil McKenzie, and two New Zealanders, Phil Bancroft and Mike Kuiti. All looked useful, in particular McKenzie, who was eventually regarded as a hooker but also played at loose forward and stand-off. Big clubs duly took note of his handling skills.

Home recruits included some very capable players, among them Kevin Harcombe, from Doncaster, who kicked a club record of 115 goals, Brian Dunn, Ian Duane and Andy Timson. Rochdale certainly brought life to the second-division scene for much of the season and were bitterly disappointed when they eventually faded out. Promotion seemed just around the corner when, like Whitehaven, they suffered a series of disasters and lost five games out of six during April to slip out of the reckoning. Following one of the defeats, at home to Keighley, their coach, Charlie Birdsall, resigned and this led to criticism of the efforts of some players in those vital matches. Hornets were disappointed with attendances after the ambition shown by the board but they had six league 'gates' of more than 1,000 during the season compared with none the previous term, when the average was only 542.

Away from the top five clubs the real success story was at Doncaster, who got rid of their joke image with a vengeance and enjoyed their best season under the two-division system with sixteen victories and a draw. Their coaches, John Sheridan and Graham Heptinstall had laid the foundations the previous year, restoring pride and enthusiasm to Tatters Field. When sponsorship money was made available for players, there were shrewd transfer dealings, among them the full-back, John Green, who made his first-division experience tell. The stand-off, Kevin Jones, looked one of the sharpest players in the league and two players broke the club try-scoring record. The prop, Kevin Parkhouse, was first with nineteen touchdowns to crown an impressive personal spell for the powerful No. 8. Then, the three-quarter, Neil Turner, from local Rugby Union, topped that tally in the final game, taking his total to twenty. Long-serving David Noble also broke his own goal-kicking record with 118.

The team's exploits in the Challenge Cup engendered much local enthusiasm and attendances in the latter part of the season were encouraging. Sheridan was rewarded by being on the short list for coach-of-the-year, a far cry from the time he took his first training session at Tatters Field and just eight players turned up and three of those were trialists.

Try-scoring records were also created at two other clubs, both by stand-offs. Bramley's Peter Lister finished with thirty-four to his credit (the previous best was only twenty). Blackpool's Tommy Frodsham also comfortably topped his club record, finishing with thirty tries, eight more than his previous best. Carlisle tried hard to make an impact and paid more than £20,000 for Bradford Northern's Dean Carroll. Sadly, achievement never quite matched ambition, though they finished with a flourish, losing only one of their last eight matches, with Gary Peacham and Kevin Pape each reaching the twenty-try mark. Carlisle also ran a second team, a praiseworthy effort, based at Penrith, and they reached the semi-finals of the Alliance Cup. The fact that almost all the players were Cumbrians raised genuine hope for the future.

Fulham played their home matches at Chiswick but again needed a last-ditch take-over to save them from extinction. Batley had their moments but the sale of Carl Gibson to Leeds lost them their prize asset. However, another young centre, Andy Williams, was full of promise and their half-back, Simon Wilson, looked a good prospect. Hunslet's Graham King registered his 100th try for the club, achieved at the commendable rate of two every three matches, and Runcorn's Brian Garrity scored twenty-four tries and Workington's David Beck twenty-three during modest seasons for their clubs.

The impression left in the second division was that the season was really three weeks too long. Too many results were embarrassing, too many teams were well below strength and standards were less than professional. The warning was clear that in some areas improvements have to be made, for clubs cannot exist for long on sentiment and sympathy.

THE PREMIERSHIP TROPHY

Patience, persistence and pack power were the principal factors that enabled Warrington to win the Slalom Lager Premiership Trophy for the first time. Persistence came in the first round when Warrington scored a last-minute try to win a tight contest against Widnes. Pack power unquestionably showed in the destruction of Wigan in the semi-final and against the champions Halifax in the final. Victory in each case was resounding. Patience belonged to the caretaker coach, Tony Barrow, for the way he had quietly rebuilt the team's confidence after the departure of Reg Bowden and the Challenge Cup defeat at Oldham. It was a notable effort by one of the game's unsung backroom men.

Three of the first-round matches went according to league placings with the home teams winning through to the semi-finals. The upset occurred at St Helens where the home side were full of confidence after thirteen successive league wins, while Leeds had just ended a run of nine games without a win by scrambling a victory at York. St Helens missed two clear-cut early chances and were made to pay for them as Leeds's skipper, Dave Heron, revelled in the firm going to create the first two tries. Suddenly Leeds were 20–8 ahead. St Helens narrowed the gap to 20–16 but Leeds brought on Paul Medley as substitute. Within three minutes he had scored and they pulled away to win comfortably, with Carl Gibson scoring two tries, including a seventy-yard effort, in a 38–22 triumph.

Hull badly needed to beat the new champions, Halifax, to salvage something from their low-key season but were always chasing a supremely confident side. The Halifax player-coach, Chris Anderson, had switched himself to the centre to give John Crossley a run at stand-off. Crossley and his scrum-half partner, Gary Stephens, dictated matters, though Chris Anderson took the try honours with two, including one from sixty yards, the sort of distance he prefers only to think about these days. Halifax were never in arrears, frequently exposing a defence that had troubled Hull all season. However, they showed they could attack and they maintained interest with two sparkling efforts: a six-man move covered seventy yards to put Garry Schofield over, and Gary Kemble and James Leuluai combined to give O'Hara a long-range score, but 32–20 was a fair reflection of Halifax superiority.

There was precious little free running in the Warrington *v.* Widnes derby at Wilderspool. Fierce tackling and hard running by Les Boyd and Kurt Sorensen were the order of the day in a tough contest. Warrington led 4–2 at the interval thanks to a penalty and two drop goals by Paul Bishop to a goal by John Myler. Widnes then forged ahead when a break by Mike O'Neill led to the ball being moved swiftly across the field for Sorensen to charge over, John Myler adding the goal. With Tony Myler always dangerous, Widnes held their advantage, despite another penalty by Bishop, until three minutes from the end. Then Billy McGinty made a break on half-way, Bishop provided the link and timed his pass perfectly to send Ronnie Duane in at the corner and Warrington had won 10–8.

The Hull KR coach, Roger Millward, picked virtually a full-strength side for the trip to Wigan, even though Wembley was six days away. Things went horribly wrong, however. Rovers were the better side early on and missed chances before Goodway sent Hanley in for the first Wigan try and Joe Lydon scored the goal. After twenty-four minutes, however, the Rovers' second-row forward, Phil Hogan, was taken off with a broken arm and the full-back, George Fairbairn, limped off with knee trouble to set the alarm bells ringing. Within a minute of the resumption, teenager Ian Lucas had scored Wigan's second try and when Rovers had their prop, Peter Johnston, sent off after fifty-one minutes they conceded the game. Wigan ran riot, with Hanley adding a hat-trick of tries in the space of five minutes, to win 47–0.

The Premiership Trophy Semi-final
Central Park, Wigan, 11 May
Wigan 12 Warrington 23

The drop goal was used to stunning effect by the Warrington stand-off, Paul Bishop, who landed five one-pointers in a marvellously competitive match. It was a classic case of the old adage, 'never leave the opposing "25" without something to show for your efforts'. Bishop was given the freedom to work his magic by the towering efforts of a splendid pack, well led by Les Boyd, in which Mark Roberts was outstanding; and by a skilled performance from the scrum-half, Andy Gregory, who showed great discipline and all his old ability.

Bishop put Warrington ahead with his first drop goal after twenty-one minutes before Gregory did supremely well to send Roberts racing over for Bishop to add the goal. Just on half-time, Wigan were given hope when brilliant handling paved the way for a try by Ian Potter, Joe Lydon adding the goal. Bishop landed two drop goals to ease Warrington clear again and then scored a splendid try after fifty-two minutes and added the goal to put his side well in command. He chipped over two more drop goals before Gregory swept through a bemused defence for a fine solo try to settle the issue.

With five minutes left, Wigan came again with a try by Ellery Hanley and Joe Lydon's second goal. But Bishop had the last word, landing a penalty to crown a great Warrington performance.

Wigan: Hampson; Lydon, Stephenson, Russell, Gill; Hanley, Edwards; Case, Kiss, Lucas, West, Potter, Goodway

Substitutes: Braithwaite for Stephenson after 53 minutes, Louw not used

Scorers: tries – Potter, Hanley; goals – Lydon (2)

Warrington: Ford; Forster, Cullen, Duane, Carbert; Bishop, Andy Gregory; Boyd, Kevin Tamati, Jackson, Sanderson, Roberts, Mike Gregory

Substitutes: Johnson for Carbert after 70 minutes, McGinty not used

Scorers: tries – Roberts, Bishop, Andy Gregory; goals – Bishop (3); drop goals – Bishop (5)

Referee: J. Holdsworth (Leeds)

Attendance: 16,639

The Premiership Trophy Semi-final
Thrum Hall, Halifax, 11 May
Halifax 16 Leeds 13

The Halifax victory summed up their season – a flat refusal to accept that the odds were piled against them. Leeds controlled a keen and at times unpleasant first half. They led 5–0 after a neat try by Norman Francis, following smart play by Hague and Keith Rayne with Hague adding a drop goal. Leeds missed other clear chances they were later to regret.

Halifax struck within two minutes of the resumption, when their substitute, Steve Bond, Gary Stephens and John Crossley combined to send Seamus McCallion over for a fine try. Colin Whitfield failed at goal but landed the penalty awarded for a foul on McCallion after he had touched down. Leeds stirred themselves and Heron and Conway led an attack which ended with Keith Rayne sending Creasser over and Conway added a touchline goal. Halifax took advantage of a Leeds handling error to reduce the arrears with a try by Tony Anderson but a penalty goal by Creasser took Leeds 13–10 ahead.

This was when Halifax showed their character, pounding the visiting line, but the weary Headingley side hung on. They kicked deep only for John Crossley to turn them with a marvellous midfield run. A penalty for obstruction on Tony Anderson, up in support, gave Halifax another footing in the Leeds '25', and with four minutes left Tony Anderson brushed off Carl Gibson to score, Whitfield adding the goal, to send Thrum Hall wild with excitement.

Halifax: Whitfield; Riddlesden, Tony Anderson, Chris Anderson, Wilson; Crossley, Stephens; Scott, McCallion, Robinson, Juliff, James, Dixon

Substitutes: Bond for Scott after 37 minutes; Steve Smith not used

Scorers: tries – McCallion, Tony Anderson (2); goals – Whitfield (2)

Leeds: Wilkinson; Francis, Creasser, Gibson, Andy Smith; Hague, Conway; Grayshon, Ward, Keith Rayne, Owen, Kevin Rayne, Heron

Substitutes: Medley for Owen at half-time, Hill for Francis after 55 minutes

Scorers: tries – Francis, Creasser; goals – Creasser, Conway; drop goal – Hague

Referee: J. McDonald (Wigan)

Attendance: 7,819

The Premiership Trophy Final
Elland Road, Leeds, 18 May
Warrington 38 Halifax 10

Warrington looked no further than their forwards to win the Premiership Trophy for the first time and their tactics paid handsome dividends in the form of a record score and record margin for the final. Warrington's Australia/New Zealand front row of Les Boyd, Kevin Tamati and Bob Jackson was awesome and there was lively support from a home-grown back three of Gary Sanderson, Mark Roberts and Mike Gregory. Halifax were crushed.

The Thrum Hall side were handicapped by an injury to Neil James, who went off after twenty-nine minutes. The surprise was that they were still level at the interval, having taken a pounding for the last twenty minutes of the first half. They owed their equality to the kicking of Colin Whitfield, who landed three fine goals, while Warrington's Paul Bishop had failed with three reasonably kickable shots.

Boyd bludgeoned over for the first try after only two minutes to give Warrington an ideal start but their defence looked uncertain early on. It was

20 One of the outstanding success stories of the season was the Australian prop, Les Boyd, at Warrington. Boyd had been out of the game for fifteen months after suspension in Australia and this was his first season in British Rugby League. He used his experience and strength to play a leading part in Warrington's crushing 38–10 victory over Halifax in the Premiership Trophy final. Here he evades the attentions of the Halifax prop, Mick Scott, in the final.

opened up by a fine pass from Gary Stephens, which enabled Paul Dixon to break clear; he judged his pass perfectly to send Chris Anderson over. Whitfield added the goal to go with an earlier well-struck penalty.

Bishop nipped over from acting half-back and at 8–8 after only twelve minutes it looked like being one of those high-scoring, 'nip-and-tuck' finals, for which the Premiership is noted. However, defences tightened and the teams were restricted to another penalty goal each before the interval, although Warrington went close when Roberts was penalized for a double move as he reached over.

Halifax blundered fatally twice within five minutes of the resumption and all at once their hopes were wrecked. First, they failed to prevent the re-starting kick going dead, giving Warrington possession in their half. The upshot was another close-in try for Kevin Tamati. Then Bishop tried a drop at goal which drifted wide of the posts but John Crossley failed to cover and Jackson plunged over for a try. At 10–22 it was virtually all over. Halifax to their credit then had their best spell of the game with Stephens, Brian Juliff and Seamus McCallion working hard but the Warrington defence held and they broke out with the best try of the match.

Andy Gregory chipped over the top, Paul Cullen swept on to the ball at speed and drew the cover to give Mark Forster the formality of completing a picture try. That certainly was the end and Halifax's weariness showed when their defence was torn apart as Warrington's substitute full-back, Brian Johnson, and Les Boyd again romped over. Boyd received the Harry Sunderland Trophy for the game's outstanding player but it could easily have gone to Kevin Tamati as these two battle-hardened warriors dominated the game.

Warrington: Ford; Forster, Cullen, Duane, Carbert; Bishop, Andy Gregory; Boyd, Kevin Tamati, Jackson, Sanderson, Roberts, Mike Gregory

Substitutes: Johnson for Ford after 22 minutes; McGinty for Sanderson after 67 minutes

Scorers: tries – Boyd (2), Bishop, Kevin Tamati, Jackson, Forster, Johnson; goals – Bishop (5)

Halifax: Whitfield; Riddlesden, Tony Anderson, Chris Anderson, Wilson; Crossley, Stephens; Scott, McCallion, Robinson, Juliff, James, Dixon

Substitutes: Bond for James after 29 minutes; Smith for Whitfield after 73 minutes

Scorers: try – Chris Anderson; goals – Whitfield (3)

Referee: F. Lindop (Wakefield)

Attendance: 13,683

Trevor Watson

5

FIVE PLAYERS OF THE SEASON

Once again selecting my five 'Players of the Season' proved easily the most difficult task of the Rugby League year and more than once involved a change of mind.

Inevitably there were candidates from Australia, though perhaps not quite as many outstanding individuals as in 1984–85. This may have been partly due to the fact that the early departure of many of them meant that they could not make an impact on some of the crucial end-of-season fixtures. Perhaps Rugby League is becoming more than ever a team game or it may be that the demands of the six-tackle rule give players less chance to star as defences continue to improve.

However, there were still many players with strong claims for selection, including a number in the second division. Steve Halliwell, Peter Lister, Tommy Frodsham, John Henderson, Kevin Parkhouse, Neil Turner and Phil McKenzie created sufficient impact to suggest they would have made an equal impression in the first division but in the end I decided to nominate only Kevin Parkhouse. Nevertheless a very useful team could have been selected to represent the second division in 1985–86 and enthusiasts might like to fill in blank winter days pondering such a choice.

Trevor Watson

Gavin Miller (Hull KR)

When Kiwi Mark Broadhurst bowed out at the end of the previous season, Hull Kingston Rovers were left with the problem of finding a pack leader of equal

21 Gavin Miller was an outstanding member of an impressive Hull KR side. It was sad that as the result of a hamstring injury just before the Challenge Cup final he was so subdued during the match that the whole team struggled as a result.

status to replace him. Surprisingly, they had little trouble, for Gavin Miller filled the breach in superb fashion.

Miller, an Australian, relatively small and stocky, does not have what is generally regarded as the tall, rangy build of a classic loose forward. But he is strong and determined and has a deceptively skilful touch, which enabled him to create chances for the eager Rovers' backs. Many of their try-scoring moves stemmed from his ability to create something out of nothing.

This was magnificently demonstrated in the Yorkshire Cup final against Castleford, when Miller was responsible for one of the great tries of the season. His strong burst gained the side a good attacking position near the touchline. This would have been success enough for most players but Miller then produced a masterly pass from the midst of a three-man tackle to send his winger, Gary Clark, clear to the line.

Miller always took a good deal of holding near the line with his ability to vary his approach in so many ways. He also had the ability to give cover and support to his scrum-half. He invariably produced his best form in big matches, taking individual awards in the county final and in the epic semi-finals against Leeds from a sizeable list of candidates. It was more than coincidence that when Miller struggled at Wembley because of hamstring trouble many of his colleagues who were perfectly fit did so too.

22 Roy Haggerty, rugged and fiercely competitive, has grown in stature since being moved into the pack from centre and enjoyed an excellent season for St Helens.

Roy Haggerty (St Helens)

This is a choice which may cause raised eyebrows among the purists. Many people believe, like me, that every side must have a battler. Saints had theirs in their second-row forward, Roy Haggerty. Still a relative light-weight, Haggerty is not everyone's idea of what a second-row forward should look like, but he has steadily developed since being moved there from centre and is vastly underrated. He is the sort of player every pack needs, with the knack of nearly always being able to find a gap in the opposing defence.

Haggerty frequently played well in big matches, making his usual breaks even when the side was in trouble and has become a much respected back-three player. He scored twenty-one tries during the season and it is an interesting

23 The much-travelled Gary Stephens joined Halifax at the beginning of the season to prove he could still do well at the highest level. He thrived on responsibility and his superb craftsmanship and organization of his forwards were important factors in the club's championship triumph.

fact that St Helens were never beaten in any club match in which he scored and that was fifteen in all.

There were times when Haggerty caught colleagues as well as opponents unprepared with his ability to slice through opposing defences, and with the right kind of support he would have set up many more tries. As it was, he beavered away, showing an abundance of spirit, and it is worth noting that he operated for lengthy spells without the team's feeder, the loose forward Harry Pinner.

Gary Stephens (Halifax)

Scrum-half Gary Stephens joined Halifax from Wigan at the start of the season well aware that he had to prove that he could still produce the goods at top level. He had played well on loan at Leigh the previous season in a struggling side but at Thrum Hall he was in a new-look team that had a question mark against it and had started badly.

The fact that Halifax went on to achieve success after success was due in no small measure to the superb craftsmanship and organization of Stephens, who never seemed to have a bad game. He thrived on responsibility and formed an excellent partnership with his player-coach, Chris Anderson, using his vast experience to great effect. Stephens was ready to organize the forwards and took on the role with skill and understanding. The fact that so many of the pack emerged as strong, direct runners, owed much to his skill as a distributor.

Like all good operators, Stephens was ready to go it alone around the scrum and at play-the-ball and added to his array of talents with some astute tactical kicking. He used the touchline in expert fashion to gain many valuable yards and, for variety, scored seven drop goals. Even when Halifax did have a bad day – which wasn't often – Stephens still played well and it is necessary to go back to his early days at Castleford to recall when he played so consistently well.

Steve Ella (Wigan)

Wigan faced a tricky situation when they signed Ellery Hanley from Bradford Northern, for they already had Steve Ella due to arrive from Australia for the stand-off position, from which Hanley had scored fifty-five tries the previous season. Ella was also used as a full-back in Australia but Wigan had no hesitation playing him at No. 6, with Hanley in the centre, and he became as popular at Central Park as Brett Kenny had been a year earlier.

Ella was another of those players to make spectators sit on the edge of their seats in anticipation of seeing something spectacular and he rarely let them down. He had lightning acceleration, which caused havoc among some defences. It was not unusual to see players preparing to make the tackle only to find that Ella was already past them, and several of his tries were scored in this way. He also had the ability to create openings for others and was prepared to draw the tackle before setting up a chance for a colleague.

His instinctive ability to follow the break was another personal quality and he worked particularly well with his fellow Australian, the prop Greg Dowling. Ella scored on his début as a substitute in the Lancashire Cup semi-final against St Helens to embark on a remarkable scoring run. He touched down in

24 Steve Ella became as popular at Central Park as Brett Kenny had been a year earlier. Wigan played Ella at stand-off and in that position he scored no less than twenty-one tries in twenty-four appearances. His pace off the mark was electrifying and he also proved himself a fine creative player.

eleven successive league and cup matches to shoot to the top of the league list despite his late start. He was hampered by injury but on his early departure had scored no less than twenty-one tries in twenty-four appearances.

Kevin Parkhouse (Doncaster)

I found this a particularly pleasing selection to make because Parkhouse played such a sizeable part in Doncaster's climb to respectability. At first glance this 17½-stone open-side prop was a throwback to days when front row men wore half-a-brick down each sock and ambled from scrum to scrum. Parkhouse certainly had his value as a scrummager, using his strength to hold the pack firm and helping to bring the best out of his hooker.

But he also used his power in open play and scored nineteen tries during the season, a tremendous tally for a No. 8, and a club record until broken again by his winger, Neil Turner, in the final game. Parkhouse did not limit his play in the loose to activity near the line; he could make breaks in midfield, showing useful speed, and was able to slip the ball to his support. He was a splendid pack leader and earned the respect of his fellow professionals. Yet this was his first full season after a spell out of the senior game, having signed for the second time during the summer of 1985 after a few appearances for Doncaster as an amateur the previous season.

Parkhouse's enthusiasm was such that he would often finish shift work down the pit and go straight on from there to training still covered in coaldust. Nor did he limit his try-scoring to the second division. Doncaster played three first-division sides in knock-out competitions and Parkhouse scored a try at St Helens, two at home to Salford and one at Leeds, leaving Tatters Field fans with the feeling that their team should have played more games against the upper crust.

25 Kevin Parkhouse scored nineteen tries during the season, a tremendous tally for a No. 8, and played a crucial part in Doncaster's climb to second-division respectability. He proved himself to be an inspired pack-leader, earning the praise of all his fellow professionals, and ended as one of the giants of the season.

6

THE AMATEUR GAME

In years to come 1985–86 will be regarded as the season in which BARLA rediscovered its sense of purpose. After a period in which internal bickering and a weak financial structure had threatened the association, BARLA, through its newly elected executive and the ever-willing national administrator, Maurice Oldroyd, silenced its critics and ended the season in better health than ever.

At the start of the season the BARLA executive decided to set itself a number of objectives in the short and medium term:

1. To gain the right for amateur teams to re-enter the Silk Cut Challenge Cup.
2. To persuade the Rugby Football Union to allow complete freedom of movement for amateur players between both codes.
3. To launch the National Amateur Rugby League.
4. To appoint a development officer for the amateur game.
5. To strengthen the finances of the association.
6. To end the dispute between BARLA and the Rugby Football League over the administration of Colts rugby.

BARLA had already taken a positive step forward at its AGM in 1985 by amending its own constitution to admit a student Rugby League representative to its executive. This was to be John Yarker, the enthusiastic organizer from Trent Polytechnic in Nottingham, already a vice-president of the British Polytechnics Sports Association. As the fastest growing section of BARLA and, many would say, the most important one, the student sector will benefit immensely from this far-sighted decision.

For several years BARLA, and in particular Maurice Oldroyd, had been lobbying the professionals to admit amateur clubs to the Challenge Cup. Though, in the past, two amateur clubs had been allowed into the competition each season in order to push numbers up to a convenient thirty-two, the expansion of the professional game in the early 1980s had put a stop to that. At last, after a skilful press campaign by BARLA, the League relented. Two BARLA clubs, Kells from Cumbria and Dudley Hill from Yorkshire, found themselves in professional company, albeit only in the preliminary round of the competition. The Cumbrians travelled to Hunslet, going down 8–20 after a creditable performance at the plush Elland Road stadium, while Dudley Hill were defeated soundly 10–38 by the 1985 finalists, Hull, at the Boulevard. Unfortunately, the preliminary round of the competition, which involved a total of eight clubs, was played on four separate dates and inevitably turned out to be something of a damp squib.

Since the formation of BARLA in 1973 the chief obstacle to the development of Rugby League has been the attitude of the Rugby Football Union, and in particular the International Board ruling that prevents a rugby player from playing both codes as an amateur if he wishes. Meetings between representatives of BARLA, leading Rugby Union officials, the Sports Council and various MPs had taken place over many years with a view to changing the rule which in its original form laid down that a player who tried his hand at Rugby League, even as an amateur, was automatically banned for life from playing Rugby Union. Although the rule had been gradually modified, the effect of it was still that an adult player, except when at college or university or in the armed services, was not allowed to play both games in the same season.

With the League game gaining in popularity in many parts of the country, it was now essential that the rule be lifted completely. Finally, after considerable pressure from the Sports Council, the RFU decided in April 1986 to recommend to its International Board that players be allowed a completely free gangway as amateur rugby players between Rugby Union and amateur Rugby League. It remains to be seen whether the International Board accepts the recommendation, but a neutral observer would think that the body would not stand in the way of such a change, especially in view of their pressing problems with professionalism generally and the possible increase in the number of 'rebel' tours to South Africa.

However, the most important development in this eventful season was the decision to form a National League of ten of the leading amateur clubs, to start in the 1986–87 season. Since its formation, BARLA's constitution has allowed for the formation of a National Premier League, but until recently the commitment of the likely contenders, both in financial and playing terms, to form a league, was in doubt.

However, the present enthusiasm in and for amateur Rugby League was seen in the response from clubs to an invitation from BARLA to apply for membership of the National League in its first year. A total of twenty-nine clubs, including South London, made formal applications. The BARLA executive members responsible for formulating the structure of the new league visited the applicants to check their facilities and assess the quality of the administration of each club. Eventually they settled on the following ten clubs: Millom and Egremont from Cumbria, Wigan St Patricks, Woolston, Pilkingtons and Leigh Miners from west of the Pennines, and West Hull, Heworth, Milford and Dudley Hill from east of the Pennines.

Inevitably at this stage of the development of the game BARLA felt unable to include a club from outside the traditional three Rugby League counties, but provision has been made for an annual system of re-election of the two clubs finishing at the bottom of the league, with other clubs having the opportunity to apply for those places. Everyone connected with BARLA hopes that in the next few years clubs outside the traditional boundaries will develop to such an extent that they are able to apply with confidence for a place in the National League.

National League matches will be played on Saturday afternoons, starting on the last Saturday in August 1986, and observers will be watching keenly to see the quality of football that the new league produces and the size of the crowds that the élite clubs attract. BARLA officials are hoping that by playing their fixtures on Saturdays the clubs will generate sufficient interest and publicity to advance the general cause of the amateur game, bringing this side of Rugby League to the attention of the general public for the first time. If BARLA can succeed in this aim there seems little doubt that they should be able to secure a lucrative sponsorship deal for the new league.

One of the chief needs of amateur Rugby League as the sport grows is more full-time workers. A specific need is that of development officers, especially in areas such as the south-west of England, where the game has made great strides. The senior vice-president of BARLA, the Cumbrian Bill Whalley, made this point forcefully in late April, when he proposed that the country be split into regions, with a development officer appointed to cover each region, though it was not clear how such a project would be financed.

However, the season did see the appointment of the first full-time development officer for Rugby League, when Leeds city council, as part of its sports development programme, appointed the Great Britain coach, Maurice Bamford, to the post of RL development officer for the council's administrative area. Bamford's infectious enthusiasm for the game quickly made its mark in the city, especially with the younger age groups, and he was able to channel boys to the established amateur clubs within the city. Although some people expressed surprise that the city of Leeds, often regarded as the centre of the game, should need a development officer, it was pointed out that the number of clubs in the city with teams at other than open-age level could be counted on the fingers of one hand. And with the decline of Rugby League in schools the need for boys to learn the game in a club context is more acute than ever.

BARLA's finances were given an encouraging boost during the season by generous grants from two metropolitan counties, which were due to be abolished at the end of March. The county councils of West Yorkshire and Greater Manchester each gave grants running into six figures for the purchase of new BARLA headquarters in Huddersfield and a centre of excellence in Leigh respectively. Undoubtedly the opportunity to move out of their present cramped premises into more spacious accommodation should enable BARLA to make at least some of the administrative appointments that are needed to ease the workload of the national administrator.

Another issue on which BARLA had hoped, but in the event failed, to make progress during the year was the difficult problem of Colts football. BARLA has always argued that the administration of Under-19 Rugby League should be left to them. They believe that Colts rugby administered by the professional clubs has weakened and, in many instances, effectively destroyed Under-19 amateur rugby in many areas. The Rugby Football League, on their side, argue that their Colts system, bringing the cream of young players together at Under-19 level within clubs, is essential in order to develop and hone the skills necessary for the professional game. The argument has rumbled on for years, with both sides now occupying entrenched positions in the dispute.

The dispute over Colts rugby is symptomatic of the dangers of having two separate organizations responsible for administering Rugby League in Great Britain. An argument that would undoubtedly be quickly settled if one body was responsible for administering the game has been allowed to simmer with no signs of a breakthrough, regardless of which body has right on its side. However, it seems unlikely that any moves towards amalgamation will be made, certainly in the short term, though the money needed for development officers, for example, might be available from the Rugby Football League if the two bodies were to merge.

On the field, the season was marked by tours from the Tweed Heads Seagulls club from northern New South Wales and the Sydney University club. The Seagulls were beaten by Lancashire and Yorkshire, before themselves defeating a BARLA President's XIII at Batley. However, the major shock of their tour was their defeat 12–13 by the Southern League, an indication of the standards currently being attained by the amateurs in and around London.

Sydney University also played the Southern League but this time the Londoners could not repeat their earlier victory, going down narrowly but giving another highly respectable performance against the more experienced Australians. Unfortunately all the other matches arranged for the University were cancelled through bad weather.

On the representative front, BARLA's annual international against France B was played at Halifax in April in front of the enthusiastic local Rugby League supporters. Against a strong French team BARLA lost 2–12 with a generally disappointing performance. The British were beaten by a team which possessed more all round skill and pace, although some of the British players betrayed a tendency to give away far too many penalties for niggling incidents, most of which were spotted by a stern referee, Robert Belle from Avignon.

The BARLA Youth team travelled to Villeneuve-sur-Lot in the same month and came away with a draw, 8–8, while other travellers to France were the British Students, who again failed to beat a strong French side, losing 8–14. Against a French team with three full internationals and a number of Under-23 internationals, the British team fielded eight players who were introduced to RL for the first time while at college or university, a remarkable indicator of the growth in the standards of representative student rugby.

The British schoolboys were also Easter visitors to France. After a well-organized preparation by the coach, Dennis McHugh, and a series of warm-up games in France, the side gained a good win against their French counterparts by 20–12, continuing the series of excellent results at Under-16 level and no doubt auguring well for the future flow of professional talent.

The major competition open to BARLA clubs, the Whitbread National Trophy, attracted a record entry of 164 teams, with entries from both the Southern League and the Midlands and South-West League. For the first time the competition was seeded, with clubs from the premier divisions of the major regional leagues being exempt until the fourth round.

Undoubtedly the team of the earlier rounds was South London, the club based at Herne Hill stadium. Drawn away to Huyton Hornets in the first round, they made the long journey to the north-west and surprised their hosts with a resounding victory by 48–8. In the second round they were at home to Todmorden from the Pennine League and again gave the northerners plenty to think about with a 38–0 victory. In the third round they were again drawn at home, and again they scored thirty-eight points, this time against Hemsworth from the Yorkshire League, who managed to score five in reply. In the fourth round they were drawn away against the mighty Leigh Miners, giving a good account of themselves and holding the Miners for much of the game before finally going down by 10–44. However, South London made history by progressing so far in the competition and defeating such strong opponents on the way. No other southern club has achieved such success in the history of BARLA, and this is surely a pointer to the future inclusion of a London-based club in the National League.

26 Consistently strong forward play by Myson's marked the final of the BARLA Whitbread National Trophy. Prop forward Tony Lamb, seen here trying to evade a tackle by the Millom stand-off, Craig Evans, demonstrated his accurate passing skills when making the third try for Myson's, scored by their winger, Stan Whittaker.

BARLA Whitbread National Trophy Final
Headingley, Leeds, 25 May
Myson's (Hull) 17 Millom 8

In a highly competitive match at Headingley, Myson's scored all but one of their points in a ten-minute spell early in the second half after containing powerful forward play from the Cumbrian-based Millom club in the first forty minutes.

Playing in front of strong support Millom led 2–1 at half-time through a penalty for offside by Bawden, Myson's replying with a drop goal by their stand-off, Sawyers. Myson's scored their first try after forty-eight minutes when Sawyers dummied and then accelerated to race in from twenty-five yards. Four minutes later their loose forward, O'Dell, chipped the ball over the Millom defence and managed to control the bouncing ball before touching down.

Soon afterwards Myson's prop forward, Lamb, who had had a strong game with his fellow prop, Crooks, sent out a long pass for the right wing, Whittaker, to score another exciting try. With man-of-the-match Sawyers converting two of the tries Myson's were virtually out of reach at 17–2 after three-quarters of the game.

However, to their credit Millom fought back, with their substitute, Evans, who came on to the field in the sixty-fifth minute, sending in Wilkinson for a try, with Bawden adding the goal. But despite Millom's superhuman efforts, Myson's defence held firm for a deserved victory.

Myson's: Kemp; Whittaker, Denman, Irwin, Taylor; Sawyers, Powley; Crooks, Owst, Lamb, Frost, Clayton, O'Dell

Substitute: Pennock for Frost after 50 minutes; Towson not used

Scorers: tries – Sawyers, O'Dell, Whittaker; goals – Sawyers (2); drop goal – Sawyers

Millom: Mawson; Mason, Bawden, Wilkinson, Robinson; Evans, O'Brien; Lawrence Lupton, Roskell, Graham Lupton, Andy Mossop, Kelly, Clive Mossop

Substitutes: Donald for Mawson after 30 minutes, Evans for Lawrence Lupton after 65 minutes

Scorers: try – Wilkinson; goals – Bawden (2)

Referee: A. Bowman (Cumbria)

Attendance: 5,000

In the outpost areas, South London were inevitably the champions of the Southern League, gaining the double with a cup final victory over St Mary's College.

In the south-west, Bath became the champions of the new league, after a remarkable season in which ten teams were regularly completing fixtures in an area completely devoid of Rugby League only two years previously.

The county cups were won by Simms Cross (Lancashire), Dudley Hill

27 The sixth Oxford v. Cambridge University Rugby League match ended in victory for Cambridge 32–14 on a cold and rainswept March night at Headingley, Leeds, thus squaring the series to date 3–3. Here James Dingemans, who represented Oxford University against Cambridge at both League and Union during the season, supports his stand-off, Chris Horner, who releases the ball despite an impending tackle by the Cambridge centre, Andrew Montgomery.

(Yorkshire), and Kells (Cumbria), with Dudley Hill and Simms Cross playing off for the right to join Kells in the preliminary round of the Silk Cut Challenge Cup.

The outstanding team in the student sector was Trent Polytechnic from Nottingham, the first Polytechnic team to become UCARLA champions after defeating Hull University in the final of the UCARLA Premiership competition at Halifax. Earlier in the season they had defeated Sheffield Polytechnic in the final of the British Polytechnics Cup with a devastating display at Sheffield.

The UCARLA Cup was won by Leeds Polytechnic, who defeated their neighbours from Bradford University in a rousing final at Headingley. Loughborough University fulfilled their promise of recent seasons by winning the UAU Trophy, and the South Glamorgan Institute of Higher Education won the competition for the British Colleges Sports Association Cup.

Sadly, the student season was marred by the death of Geoff Peggs, the British Students coach, after a long illness. A strong believer in the importance of student rugby, Peggs had been a great servant of UCARLA and his loss was a blow, particularly in view of the imminence of a student world cup, due to take place in New Zealand in August 1986.

Martyn Sadler

7

RUGBY LEAGUE'S CHALLENGE

I think it best to come clean from the outset. I have only seen a handful of Rugby League games, one of which was the 1985 Challenge Cup final between Wigan and Hull. A contest that was so enthralling, so exciting, so full of skill and imagination that I was moved to write that it was better than the Barbarians versus the All Blacks classic at the Arms Park in those heady days of 1973 when British Rugby Union, for once, stood supreme.

You may have discerned that I have a lingering affection for Rugby Union. This is hardly surprising as it was the winter game I was forced to play for seven years while at grammar school. It seems strange, in retrospect, that my sporting education was so restricted. Today, our children are exposed to any number of sports and leisure activities. This has meant that our traditional sports – soccer, rugby and cricket – have suffered. Unlike most diehards who consider this to be further diminution of our sporting heritage, I have supported it, for I'm sure the future of all sports lies outside the school curriculum.

Incidentally, another abiding memory of the 1985 Challenge Cup final was the Under-11 match that preceded it. It was simply brilliant. If I'd been given the opportunity to play at Wembley at that age, I'd have thought Christmas had come early. What an experience: seeing it for the first time made me realize that mini-rugby is a bastard game and should be replaced immediately in all schools by its Rugby League counterpart.

Anyway, as anyone interested in Rugby League will know, the principal challenge facing the game is how to induce more people to play it and more people to watch it. Well, to start with, the continuing conflict between Rugby League and Union this last season has at least won for RL a hugely sympathetic press. It began innocently enough in an article I wrote in *Open Rugby* in which I advised BARLA to sue the RFU over the issue of players being allowed freedom of access to play either amateur code any time, any place.

Ironically, the students at Oxford – as in other universities, colleges and polytechnics – have been allowed to play both Rugby League and Union for a year or two without receiving a visit from the heavy brigade at Twickenham. It is only when they become fully fledged adults that the players are prevented from walking off one pitch on to another. Extraordinary: but there will soon be change. Perhaps my remarks in *Open Rugby* may have helped, in some small way, to end the conflict for, quite suddenly, in April the RFU agreed to recommend to the next meeting of the International Board that there should be a 'free gangway' between the two amateur codes. Incidentally, with sport in higher education generally in disarray, Rugby League has prospered because it is administered by a single body (UCARLA) and not organized on the old separate lines of university, polytechnic and college. Mind you, apart from the South Glamorgan Institute of Higher Education, most of the top teams are based in the north. Indeed, Rugby League really does need a strong base in clubs and colleges south of Watford if it is truly going to become a national, and then an international, sport.

BARLA's aim is to have an amateur Rugby League club in every major city and town before the centenary of its birth is celebrated in 1995. This is a tall order. At the moment, the Southern League (where four-fifths of the population reside) has a mere twenty-one teams of which fourteen are in London. Indeed, as Ealing, Streatham Celtic, Fulham Amateurs and Hemel Hempstead field two teams, the actual number of clubs is as low as seventeen.

A glance at the Midland and South-West League table reveals much the same story. Ten teams play but as Wokingham also feature in the London table and Cheltenham have two clubs the game can hardly be said to have taken root. Now, all these developments may be new and exciting, the more so if you consider our inherently reactionary nature to sporting change, but they're hardly earth shattering.

Moreover, the proposed National Premier League, while ambitious, will again focus attention on clubs in the north. I'm not sure this is the way to encourage its growth nationwide. Aside from Cheltenham and possibly Milton Keynes, I doubt if there is a club south of a line from The Wash to Bristol that will be able to meet, for another decade, the fierce criteria laid down by BARLA.

I think the principal question that needs to be resolved is which is the best way to foster the game in the Midlands and in the south and south-west of the country, given the healthy respect for Rugby Union there. In an ideal world, it would be possible for Union and League teams to share the same facilities. Indeed, my instincts are that where Union clubs enjoy the patronage of local authorities, the right to equal facilities for a League club could be tested in the courts.

It's not just a matter of ensuring that Rugby League is on every secondary school curriculum. School sport cannot survive in its present form. I'd prefer it to be taken out of school altogether. I mean the very notion that a physical education teacher can be proficient in the eighteen sports that make up track and field, or be competent at coaching netball or archery or gymnastics, to any worthwhile standard, is clearly ludicrous. All that wider choice has provided, under the umbrella of physical 'education', is an *hors d'œuvre* philosophy – pick here, pick there and, as long as you're not hungry, that's fine. But, if you are, tough. It will become harder for any child to aspire to excellence in sport over the next decade. And this attitude is relevant to the debate about Rugby League in the south.

Given that school sport as you and I understood it has changed, and given that the present government has even sold off school playing-fields, the future of all sport is with the local sports centre. Sports centres could so quickly be linked into a national system. So Rugby League needs to re-align itself with its sports centres. This won't happen overnight. But, within a year or two, they could become a focus for the game and facilities will then *have* to be provided.

In conjunction with this development, clubs in the south need to be twinned with clubs in the north (they might even share the same name); for example, Bexleyheath might be twinned with Leeds. This would mean that Bexleyheath would be able to watch, train and be supervised by the Leeds club, say once a month, at Headingley. It would also be necessary for Leeds to visit Bexleyheath, its sports centres and schools to give teach-ins and foster a healthier attitude to the game. I suspect a sponsor might be even more interested in a major club, if he could also see that his name would become known in another part of the country. It wouldn't be long before Bexleyheath's sports centres would be challenging Leeds' sports centres to badminton, squash, soccer, swimming and Rugby League in a festival weekend. Such an exchange could only be beneficial to sport as a whole and to League in particular.

Two further areas need to be examined if League is to become a national game within ten years. The first is that coaching courses need to be organized outside of Bolton, Bradford, Calderdale, Cheshire, Humberside, Kirklees, Leeds, Rochdale, St Helens, Salford, Sheffield, Stockport, Wakefield, Wigan and York.

More important, the way Rugby League is portrayed on television needs a long, hard look. BBC sport is not what it was. It has become complacent – its directors and producers have had tennis, golf, cricket and rugby for so long that they have lost their creative urge. Channel 4, under the brilliant stewardship of Adrian Metcalfe, has demonstrated again and again through its fresh approach to American Football, cricket from Australia, basketball and volleyball that there are alternative ways of portraying sport.

Live coverage of a game on a Saturday afternoon does no one any favours, least of all rugby followers. The game needs a one hour spot on a Monday evening. Like American Football, the viewer wants to see highlights from the best weekend game or games. So Monday evening could be given over to an appraisal of the weekend's play and include live coverage of a game held over from Sunday. The current presentation is devoid of life. Eddie Waring, bless him, went on too long and in the end became a kind of music-hall joke. Bill McLaren is in danger of doing the same for Rugby Union. It would be a sad day if Ray French was to follow suit. None the less, the way in which League is presented is critical to the expansionist activities of BARLA. Five years ago you'd have slipped down to the local rather than watch snooker, darts, bowls, *Ski-Sunday*, American Football or baseball. Yet they have marketed themselves to such an extent that we're staying in and brewing our own!

I've said enough. Well, nearly enough. Rugby League is an infinitely more skilful game than Rugby Union, except for that mess called a scrum. Union is dying on its feet; by that I mean, it's still popular as a game but technically and tactically it is bereft of creative thinkers at the centre of its administration. Sadly, Twickenham pays homage only to yesterday's men.

Derek Wyatt

8

REFLECTIONS

An historian setting out to chronicle the events of the 1985–86 season would have to be prepared to write a multi-volume work, so full and frenetic was the activity on and off the field, especially during the last six weeks of the season. After the New Zealand Tests and some marvellous cup matches, and as a result of the changes in the structure of the game that have sprung from innumerable meetings and discussions off the field, I am now much more confident that representatives of clubs on the various organizing bodies of the game have a greater awareness of the needs of the sport as a whole, have relaxed their largely parochial attitudes, and have come up with some really interesting and constructive ideas. Those ideas, some revolutionary, others simply confirming the gradual working out of the League's thinking over recent years, may have far-reaching consequences, helping to fashion a truly national game from Rugby League before the celebration of its centenary in 1995.

Spectators at this year's replayed Silk Cut Challenge Cup semi-final between Leeds and Hull KR, and those supporters who braved the rain and cold at the Widnes *v.* Wigan league fixture, will confirm my view that the game at top professional level has greatly improved. The commitment in the tackling, the support play, the tactical kicking and the individual skills in those and many other matches made me believe that we had emerged at last from the trough of despair following the Australian tour in 1982. And proposals for the restructuring of the professional game, coupled with the strengthening of the Alliance League, gives the game a broader base for further development.

The decisions to reduce the first division to fourteen clubs at the start of the 1987–88 season; to reduce to eight per cent the levy payable by all first-division clubs to the League's central funds, with no share-out among clubs at the end of the season; and to increase the share of the Challenge Cup 'gate' for the two finalists from ten to fifteen per cent, are sure to lift the game's playing standards by providing hard-pressed clubs with more much-needed income. No doubt any reorganization of the second division will be based (in the short term) on regional east and west fixture-lists but I feel sure that in due course this will evolve naturally into three divisions where right of entry is determined by merit. Such a structure will provide a much greater incentive to clubs to foster the Alliance League whose success was a major feature of the 1985–86 season. The decision to arrange play-offs between the top teams in the second division at the end of the season should also be applauded.

Though Hull experienced a mediocre season by their standards, failing to gain a single trophy, there was no denying the success of the Hull team which won the Alliance League championship. Though renowned as a side never afraid to bring the best of overseas talent to Humberside, Hull are wisely supporting the new Alliance venture, still only in its second season, as a nursery for young players. Swinton, too, despite being relegated to the second division, amply illustrated their faith in Alliance rugby and reaped the rewards by recording an 18–16 win over Leeds in the Slalom Lager Alliance Cup final at Headingley. The lowly Penrith–Carlisle side, in reaching the semi-final of the Cup competition, also indicated what a valuable outlet for young talent an Alliance side is as well as enabling the Carlisle club itself to develop their ex-Cumbrian amateur talent together in one team.

Until the formation of the Alliance League at the beginning of the 1984–85 season, 'A' team football was threatened with extinction as clubs failed to raise sides and continually cried off fixtures with the flimsiest excuse. Not so now, and especially following the injection of £15,000 of sponsorship money by the brewers Matthew Brown. The attitude to Alliance League rugby is best illustrated by the fact that many clubs now desperately wish to be included in the league; Rochdale Hornets, for example, played friendly matches against Alliance opposition as a prelude to seeking entry themselves for 1986–87. The fact that Keighley, who failed to win a single match throughout the season and suffered a points tally of 1069 against, still managed to fulfil all their twenty-six Alliance fixtures speaks volumes not only for the Yorkshire club but for the success of the competition itself. Most clubs now let their younger players develop gradually and find the Alliance team a good introduction for trialists whether they be from League or Union.

A glance at the youngsters being developed in professional Colts rugby also shows that British talent is once again being fostered at an early age. But not all senior clubs are happy with the present structure. After watching a number of Colts matches, in particular the Wigan *v.* Hull KR Colts Premiership final, played prior to the Premiership final itself, I have no doubt that a club with a youth team is well qualified to develop the skills of young players of quality. Indeed, when Wigan can include Ian Lucas, Martin Dermott, and Richard

Russell, all players with considerable first-team experience, in their Colts team few can argue with that point of view. However, the dispute, which once again rumbled on throughout the season, is about whether young players' skills should be developed by a professional club or by BARLA.

Many consider that the Rugby League, by subsidizing the Colts League to the extent of £20,000 a season, is damaging BARLA's own efforts to promote youth rugby. Many are outraged at the money being used to subsidize Colts teams at professional clubs when the young players could be produced at no cost in the amateur leagues. Many professional clubs run Colts teams and Wigan, St Helens, Castleford, and Leeds, especially, speak highly of the value of their production line of talent. Yet other clubs, the most notable being Widnes, have little use for a Colts set-up, preferring to buy their players from the local amateur youth leagues. Angry words have been spoken at periodic intervals throughout the season as advocates of each system have lobbied for support.

The test of the Colts League's true merits and the intentions of the professional clubs can surely be determined by the withdrawal of the subsidy or its transfer to the Alliance League. Why should a subsidy be granted to some clubs who wish to run a Colts team and no payments be made to those clubs who do not? Perhaps a share of the subsidy could be paid to all clubs, leaving each club to determine its priorities. Thus if a club felt it was beneficial to them to run a Colts team, they might create one; if a club felt it was not to their advantage, they might use their money, for example, to sign amateur players.

The other protagonist in this seemingly endless controversy, BARLA, can look back on the season as another in which they have made remarkable progress towards their ideal of a truly national amateur sport. The announcement of the ten clubs who are to contest their newly-created National League in 1986–87 will form the apex of the BARLA structure and will no doubt act as the 'flagship' of amateur Rugby League. Such a league will act as an incentive to the new amateur sides springing up in London, the south-west, Wales, the Midlands and the south-east. However, the most far-reaching announcement came from Twickenham, the implications of which could be huge. Whether suffering embarrassment over the Steve Ford affair, when the Cardiff wing was banned from playing Rugby Union by the Welsh RU, following the revelations of an RL trial with Leeds, or because of continuing heavy pressure from representatives of the Sports Council, the Rugby Football Union announced that they would recommend to the International Board a 'free gangway' between the two amateur codes. The timing of this proposal, coming after years of fruitless, often acrimonious discussion, took everyone by surprise. Now I firmly believe that, with the RFU beset by the mounting problem of professionalism, such an agreement (assuming the International Board accepts that recommendation) may mark the beginning of a new era in the development of Rugby League in this country – if BARLA and Chapeltown Road seize the opportunity.

If some form of professional Rugby Union springs from New Zealand's renegade tour of South Africa in the summer of 1986, it could have a dramatic effect on RL's intake of new players, especially at youth level. The number of ex-Union players coming into League may well dry up if a young man is able to live near home, keep his normal job and yet be paid a reasonable wage and generous expenses for playing Rugby Union.

With what inducements will League be able to tempt the future equivalents of Billy Boston, Tom Van Vollenhoven, David Watkins and so on to change from professional Rugby Union to Rugby League? It is imperative that as a matter of urgency Rugby League redoubles its efforts to find and nurture its own talent through BARLA and through the professional clubs. We must certainly spread the League code at amateur level even faster than BARLA has done over the past ten seasons. If organized professional Rugby Union becomes a reality then, at a comparatively early age, youngsters will be given a clear choice between the two codes. It should not be difficult for a promising young player to decide which of the two codes provides the better, faster, and more skilful game, but we must be ready to give him the opportunity to choose and to reward him properly.

In the meantime, it may be significant that during the season, after a lean period for RU signings caused no doubt by lack of employment opportunities in the north and by the decline in standards of the four home unions, we experienced four major signings from Rugby Union. The arrival of Terry Holmes, the Welsh RU captain, at Bradford Northern staggered the sporting world. Though Bradford's £80,000 outlay could not be recouped last season because of Holmes's shoulder injury, his signing heralded those of the Springbok RU internationals Ray Mordt and Rob Louw, who joined their fellow South African, Nick Du Toit, at Wigan and of another ex-British Lion, Robert Ackerman, at Whitehaven. Holmes, Mordt, Louw and Ackerman, the biggest signings to come from Rugby Union for many years, may be the forerunners of several more. I envisage clubs, now bolstered by successful sponsorship deals, to be more willing than in the recent past to risk considerable cash outlay on a Union player in return for six or seven seasons' service, not simply one season as in the case of an Australian or New Zealand import. In view of Rugby Union's problems with its own rampant professionalism at the higher levels of the game, and the modern relaxed attitude of society to professionalism, I believe that the stigma of signing for a League club, once so dreaded by a Union player, will hold few fears. But the real conflict lies ahead: how should we meet the challenge of professional Rugby Union if that comes about?

28 Nick Du Toit was already established at Central Park when he was joined by his fellow South Africans, the Springbok internationals Ray Mordt and Rob Louw. Though in and out of the team through injury, the hard-working Du Toit could always be relied on for a hundred per cent effort and even played at full-back in an emergency.

If last season's activity off the field is to the advantage of the League code I believe that, on the field, playing skills have evolved in a fashion far removed from my own playing days. In no way do I decry the modern game for I believe that teams are now playing rugby equal to any accepted standards of the past in both attack and defence. Yes, in defence, for, having been most scathing of the art of tackling in my chapter 'Reflections' in last year's *Rugby League Review* I must say how much I admired the defensive abilities of teams like Wigan, Warrington, Hull KR and Halifax during this past season. But I must ask the question: 'Where have all the wingers and props gone?'

In a game renowned for its wing play, with memories of legendary wingers like Alf Ellaby, Eric Harris, Albert Rosenfeld, Tom Van Vollenhoven, Billy Boston, Mick Sullivan, and Brian Bevan, we now have a dearth of top-class wingers. We see excellent players like Joe Lydon (Wigan) and Carl Gibson (Leeds) alternating between wing and centre positions. Des Drummond (Leigh) has few challengers for his Great Britain place and a look at the top ten try-scorers for the season reveals the names of only two wingers – Phil Fox (Leigh) and Carl Gibson. The remaining eight are midfield players with the top two proving that big centres are now the important players in a three-quarter line. Perhaps Gary Prohm (Hull KR), with his forty-five tries in the 1984–85 season, set the trend. It is a trend which saddens me, for there is still no finer sight on a rugby field than a fast wing racing down the touchline, tacklers clutching despairingly at his ankles.

Though intending no slight on their abilities as prop forwards, since both had particularly good playing seasons, it is a sad state of affairs when Jeff Grayshon (Leeds) and Trevor Skerrett (Hull) are included in the Great Britain summer squad to prepare for the coming Tests against Australia. Both are veterans of many campaigns, both were in the 1982 Test disasters against the Australians, yet four years later our stock of prop forwards is evidently so low that Maurice Bamford includes them in his plans. John Fieldhouse had a marvellous Test series against New Zealand in the prop position and Lee Crooks threatens to emerge as a prop of distinction, but where are the rest? Maurice Bamford's scouts must be working overtime to find them.

At the time of the change to the limited-tackle count, and especially since the introduction of the six-tackle rule, Rugby League has become obsessed with speed. 'There will be fewer scrums, all the forwards must run like stags,' has been the cry. Clubs have become so obsessed with pace that they have forgotten the big props who are so necessary in midfield, and they have also ignored the fact that many big men can run. Australia can still assemble players like Craig Young, Greg Dowling, or Les Boyd for a forward battle. But, in Britain, the lack of prop forwards has obviously been accentuated by the sharp reduction in scrums in a modern game. From a count of forty scrums in a match we have now declined to an average of fifteen with, I believe, a resultant decline in combined midfield back play and the neglect, as I previously indicated, of wingers.

In a John Player Special Trophy match between Halifax and Hull KR the sight of George Fairbairn linking up with his centre, Mike Smith, following a quick pass by Paul Harkin from the base of a successful scrum, amply illustrated the ploys which can occur behind the scrummage. Swinton in the 1960s, with a midfield trio of Buckley, Fleet, and Rhodes, developed set-piece play to a fine art and cultivated the wing skills of the highly-talented John Stopford. Though I am unlikely ever to see a return to the number of scrums of past years I would like to see coaches encouraging their scrum-half to initiate moves from behind the scrum. With each midfield player harnessing his skills to that of the others, those sudden defence-splitting moves can bring a crowd to its feet and, above all, provide the space for a wing to employ his talents. We could see wingers restored to their rightful positions in the try-scoring charts.

It is more than possible that it was because of the present decline in wing play, overseas as well as in Britain, that no club last season offered terms to an Australian or New Zealand wing, though we again experienced an influx of overseas stars. With a reduction in the quota of imported players, clubs tended to be more selective than in the previous season when anyone with an Australian accent was considered. Players like Steve Ella, Greg Dowling, Noel Cleal, Joe Kilroy, Cavill Heugh and Geoff Robinson were supreme entertainers at Wigan, Widnes and Halifax whilst St Helens were overjoyed at the pace and future promise of the young Kiwi centre, Mark Elia. As last season, such players did attract the crowds but, with the import quota due for a further drop in 1987–88 to an allowance of three players per club, I suspect that clubs will once again turn their attention to the traditional recruiting grounds of Rugby Union.

In conclusion, I must emphasize that this season has made me genuinely optimistic about standards of coaching. The days when a club's directors picked a famous player as their coach, irrespective of his coaching ability, and then sat back to see if he would make the grade are happily a thing of the past. The endless nights of touch rugby and slow laps round the training area no longer win the trophies in Rugby League. At last there are signs that the coaching policies devised by Phil Larder, Les Bettinson and the area coaching staffs are paying dividends. And the Australian influence is also beginning to have a good effect behind the scenes. Though eleven club coaches chose not to attend an end-of-season weekend seminar, where soccer managers, psychiatrists, and physical education experts offered their advice and experience, the result of the emphasis on new methods in training is evident.

Serious thinkers on the game like Roger Millward and Mal Reilly won success for Hull KR and Castleford while the Wigan club, though missing out on the Championship and Challenge Cup, enjoyed considerable success under Colin Clarke and Alan McInnes. All four of these coaches were heavily influenced by Australian methods. Yet the success of Halifax in winning the first-division championship and Warrington's triumph in the Premiership play-offs are indications of a trend which I believe will develop over the next few seasons. Our game has welcomed Australian players and Australian training methods. In Chris Anderson (the Halifax player-coach) and Les Boyd (who became the assistant player-coach at Warrington) I believe we have seen some of our top clubs beginning to realize that an Australian coach might be the best signing of all. Chris Anderson blended his Australian and British players at Halifax into a formidable team whose strength was based in defence. Les Boyd ably assisted Warrington's caretaker coach, Tony Barrow, in the final eight weeks of the season and proved the value of his direction on the field. The news that Wigan have attracted a coach of the calibre of Graham Lowe, the national coach of New Zealand, is further evidence of this welcome trend.

Though the vote at the end of the season to refuse Stockport County admission to the Rugby League was, for me, a backward decision, I think we can look on 1985–86 as a season when the League code made great strides forward. At last administrators with a broader vision are coming to the front and, though not yet dominant, are nudging our game ever so slowly in a new and more positive direction.

Ray French

Appendix 1

THE KIWI TOUR OF GREAT BRITAIN AND FRANCE

Results in Great Britain

6 October: v. Wigan Lost 8–14 Attendance 12,856

9 October: v. Great Britain Under-21 (at Odsal Stadium, Bradford) Won 16–12 Attendance 2,285

13 October: v. Hull Kingston Rovers Won 20–10 Attendance 6,585

15 October: v. Cumbria (at Whitehaven) Won 32–6 Attendance 5,500

19 October: v. Great Britain **First Test** (at Headingley, Leeds) Won 24–22 Attendance 12,591

23 October: v. Yorkshire (at Odsal Stadium, Bradford) Lost 8–18 Attendance 3,745

27 October: v. St Helens Won 46–8 Attendance 7,897

29 October: v. Leeds Won 16–10 Attendance 4,713

2 November: v. Great Britain **Second Test** (at Central Park, Wigan) Lost 8–25 Attendance 15,506

4 November: v. Widnes Won 32–12 Attendance 5,200

9 November: v. Great Britain **Third Test** (at Elland Road, Leeds) Draw 6–6 Attendance 22,209

13 November: v. Lancashire (at Watersheddings, Oldham) Cancelled – heavy frost

17 November: v. Hull Won 33–10 Attendance 8,500

The Kiwi Tour of Great Britain and France

Results in France

November 20: v. Invitation XIII (at Paris) Won 20–8 Attendance 1,500

November 23: v. France **First Test** (at Marseilles) Won 22–0 Attendance 1,500

November 27: v. Midi/Pyrénées Selection (at Toulouse) Won 18–12 Attendance 2,000

November 29: v. Languedoc/Roussillon Selection (at Carcassonne) Won 66–1 Attendance 3,000

December 1: v. Rest of the World Selection (at Narbonne) Won 22–10 Attendance 700

December 4: v. Aquitaine/Provence–Côte d'Azur Selection (at Talence) Won 22–10 Attendance 1,930

December 7: v. France **Second Test** (at Perpignan) Won 22–0 Attendance 3,045

Totals: Played 19, Won 15, Drew 1, Lost 3
Points for 441 Points against 194

Team statistics

	Played	*Tests*	*Tries*	*Goals*	*Points*
Fred Ah Kuoi	5	5	—	—	—
Dean Bell	13	5	4	—	16
Mark Bournville	12	—	4	—	16
Shane Cooper	12	1	2	—	8
Ricky Cowan	7	1	—	—	—
Martin Crequer**	5	—	3	1	14
Mark Elia	14	1	12	—	48
Olsen Filipaina	15	5	2	35	78
Clayton Friend	12	5	7	—	28
Glen Gibb	6	—	1	—	4
James Goulding	8	1	—	—	—
Mark Graham*	4	2	3	—	12
Shane Horo	9	—	7	—	28
Gary Kemble	5	5	1	—	4
James Leuluai	5	5	1	—	4
Hugh McGahan	12	5	6	—	24
Vaun O'Callaghan	6	—	2	7	22
Dane O'Hara	5	5	2	—	8
Ron O'Regan	11	1	3	—	12
Gary Prohm	3	3	—	—	—
Joe Ropati*	6	—	—	8	16
Adrian Shelford	11	—	2	—	8
Dane Sorensen	9	5	—	4	8
Kurt Sorensen	11	5	5	—	20
Sam Stewart	11	1	5	—	20
Howie Tamati	10	2	1	—	4
Kevin Tamati	3	2	—	—	—
Ross Taylor*	3	—	1	—	4
Brent Todd**	7	1	1	—	4
Wayne Wallace	9	3	1	—	4
Graeme West	2	1	—	—	—
Darrel Williams	13	2	2	—	8
Owen Wright	12	3	2	5 + 1 drop goal	19
Totals:			80	60 + 1 drop goal	441

* Returned home injured
** Replacements for injured players

Appendix 2

THE JOHN PLAYER SPECIAL TROPHY

Preliminary round

Featherstone R.	10	Warrington	14
West Hull	10	Castleford	24
Keighley	24	Jubilee (Featherstone)	6
Carlisle	6	Rochdale H.	24

1st round

Fulham	13	Warrington	20
Barrow	5	Leeds	2
Blackpool B.	22	Wakefield T.	24
Wigan	26	Mansfield M.	0
Whitehaven	7	Widnes	12
Sheffield E.	16	Bradford N.	24
Batley	2	Leigh	70
Hunslet	20	Workington T.	12
Halifax	2	Hull KR	11
Bramley	8	Oldham	46
York	12	Castleford	10
Keighley	20	Huddersfield B.	10
St Helens	42	Dewsbury	6
Doncaster	22	Runcorn H.	20
Hull	44	Swinton	0
Salford	18	Rochdale H.	10

2nd round

Warrington	34	Barrow	14
Wakefield T.	21	Wigan	30
Widnes	30	Bradford N.	6
Leigh	48	Hunslet	6
Hull KR	8	Oldham	7
York	21	Keighley	16
St Helens	36	Doncaster	20
Hull	30	Salford	10

The John Player Special Trophy

3rd round		*Semi-finals*		*Final*	
Warrington	22				
		Wigan	36		
Wigan	26				
				Wigan	11
Widnes	31				
		Leigh	8		
Leigh	35				
Hull KR	24				
		Hull KR	22		
York	16				
				Hull KR	8
St Helens	57				
		St Helens	4		
Hull	14				

Appendix 3

THE JOHN SMITH'S YORKSHIRE CUP

1st round		*2nd round*		*Semi-finals*		*Final*	
Hull KR	12	Hull KR	30	Hull KR	11	Hull KR	22
Hull	10						
Bramley	22	Bramley	6				
Doncaster	10						
York	18	Featherstone R.	11	Bradford N.	5		
Featherstone R.	26						
Bradford N.	40	Bradford N.	22				
Wakefield T.	15						
Batley	10	Dewsbury	2	Leeds	10	Castleford	18
Dewsbury	14						
Leeds	60	Leeds	48				
Keighley	12						
Halifax	52	Halifax	4	Castleford	14		
Huddersfield B.	14						
Castleford	60	Castleford	24				
Hunslet	2						

Appendix 4

THE BURTONWOOD BREWERY LANCASHIRE CUP

1st round		*2nd round*		*Semi-finals*		*Final*	
Wigan	24	Wigan	22	Wigan	30	Wigan	34
Fulham	13						
Salford	18	Salford	20				
Swinton	14						
St Helens	72	St Helens	26	St Helens	2		
Carlisle	8						
Barrow	8	Whitehaven	8				
Whitehaven	12						
Warrington	30	Warrington	38	Warrington	11	Warrington	8
Blackpool B.	3						
Runcorn H.	16	Workington T.	4				
Workington T.	38						
Leigh	40	Leigh	14	Widnes	4		
Oldham	12						
Rochdale H.	6	Widnes	18				
Widnes	17						

Appendix 5

THE SILK CUT CHALLENGE CUP

Preliminary round

Hunslet	20
Kells	8
Carlisle	26
Mansfield M.	14
Hull	38
Dudley Hill	10
Swinton	8
Leeds	30

1st round

Workington T.	12
Wigan	56
Dewsbury	19
St Helens	29
Fulham	14
Barrow	26
Hunslet	6
Castleford	60
Oldham	56
Carlisle	10
Warrington	62
Sheffield E.	11
Bradford N.	10
Wakefield T.	8
Bramley	8
Batley	6
York	18
Whitehaven	6
Hull KR	22
Hull	6
Keighley	2
Leigh	24
Blackpool B.	30
Runcorn H.	10
Featherstone R.	14
Widnes	18
Huddersfield B.	4
Rochdale H.	10
Doncaster	18
Salford	12
Halifax	4
Leeds	24

2nd round

Wigan	24
St Helens	14
Barrow	6
Castleford	30
Oldham	13
Warrington	6
Bradford N. (replay: 36–2 to Bradford N.)	20
Bramley	20
York	6
Hull KR	34
Leigh	31
Blackpool B.	10
Widnes	36
Rochdale H.	20
Doncaster	10
Leeds	28

3rd round		*Semi-finals*		*Final*	
Wigan	2				
Castleford	10	Castleford	18		
Oldham	6			Castleford	15
Bradford N.	1	Oldham	7		
Hull KR	25				
Leigh	10	Hull KR	24		
		(replay: 17–0 to Hull KR)		Hull KR	14
Widnes	10				
(replay: 5–0 to Leeds)		Leeds	24		
Leeds	10				

Appendix 6

THE SLALOM LAGER CHAMPIONSHIP FINAL LEAGUE TABLES

Division 1

					Points		
	P	W	L	D	F	A	Pts
Halifax	30	19	6	5	499	365	44
Wigan	30	20	3	7	776	300	43
St Helens	30	20	2	8	730	503	42
Warrington	30	20	1	9	665	393	41
Widnes	30	19	3	8	520	454	41
Leeds	30	15	3	12	554	518	33
Hull Kingston Rovers	30	16	1	13	507	498	33
Hull	30	15	2	13	616	508	32
Oldham	30	13	4	13	524	549	30
Salford	30	14	—	16	508	561	28
Castleford	30	12	1	17	551	585	25
Bradford Northern	30	11	1	18	445	474	23
Featherstone Rovers	30	9	3	18	419	616	21
York	30	9	—	21	413	592	18
Swinton	30	8	—	22	371	648	16
Dewsbury	30	5	—	25	313	847	10

Division 2

					Points		
	P	W	L	D	F	A	Pts
Leigh	34	33	—	1	1156	373	66
Barrow	34	27	—	7	1012	398	54
Wakefield Trinity	34	24	1	9	680	435	49
Whitehaven	34	22	—	12	619	479	44
Rochdale Hornets	34	21	—	13	763	485	42
Blackpool Borough	34	20	—	14	769	570	40
Batley	34	18	3	13	567	450	39
Bramley	34	17	1	16	608	663	35
Fulham	34	16	1	17	679	709	33
Doncaster	34	16	1	17	611	650	33
Carlisle	34	15	2	17	585	682	32
Sheffield Eagles	34	14	1	19	516	617	29
Workington Town	34	13	—	21	684	723	26
Hunslet	34	11	3	20	594	795	25
Huddersfield	34	8	4	22	542	841	20
Runcorn Highfield	34	9	2	23	489	790	20
Keighley	34	9	2	23	401	918	20
Mansfield Marksman	34	2	1	31	383	1080	5

Appendix 7

THE SLALOM LAGER PREMIERSHIP TROPHY

1st round		*Semi-finals*		*Final*	
Wigan	47	Wigan	12	Warrington	38
Hull KR	0				
Warrington	10	Warrington	23		
Widnes	8				
Halifax	32	Halifax	16	Halifax	10
Hull	20				
St Helens	22	Leeds	13		
Leeds	38				

Appendix 8

LEADING SCORERS

Tries

Halliwell (Leigh)	49
Hanley (Wigan)	38
Lister (Bramley)	34
Henderson (Leigh)	31
Frodsham (Blackpool B.)	30
Fox (Leigh)	29
Williams (Barrow)	27
Garrity (Runcorn H.)	24
Gibson (Leeds)	23
Beck (Workington T.)	23

Goals

Chris Johnson (Leigh)	173
Stephenson (Wigan)	128
Noble (Doncaster)	118
Harcombe (Rochdale H.)	115
Kilner (Bramley)	110
Dorahy (Hull KR)	101
Woods (Bradford N.)	98
Creasser (Leeds)	84
Carroll (Carlisle)	83
Smith (Workington T.)	83

Points

	Trs	*Gls*	*Dr.Gls*	*Pts*
Chris Johnson (Leigh)	14	171	2	400
Stephenson (Wigan)	18	126	2	326
Woods (Bradford N.)	13	97	1	247
Noble (Doncaster)	3	112	6	242
Dorahy (Hull KR)	8	99	2	232
Kilner (Bramley)	3	110	–	232

The publication of this book has been made possible through the generosity of Shopacheck Financial Services Ltd, Haltemprice Court, 38 Springfield Way, Anlaby, Hull.